JOHN WIMBER'S TEACHING ON CHURCH PLANTINIG

A Resume, by

Derek Morphew

PUBLICATION DETAILS

Vineyard International Publishing
84 Starke Road, Bergvliet, 7945, South Africa
Copyright © Derek J Morphew 2020

All rights reserved. No part of this publication may be reproduced, stored in a retrieval system or transmitted, in any form or by any means, electronic, mechanical, photocopying, recording, or otherwise, without the prior written permission of the copyright owner.

Use of the material by John Wimber was obtained from the Association of Vineyard Churches, USA, who are the owners of the copyright for the John Wimber archives.

Scripture quotations, unless otherwise specified are taken from The Holy Bible, New International Version® NIV®
Copyright © 1973 1978 1984 2011 by Biblica, Inc. TM
Used by permission. All rights reserved worldwide.

ISBN: 9798605105084

TABLE OF CONTENTS

FOREWORD BY STEVE NICHOLSON 4

INTRODUCTION 6

WHY PLANT NEW CHURCHES? 8

CHURCH PLANTING MODELS 22

THE CHURCH PLANTERS PROFILE 25

DEMOGRAPHIC RESEARCH: TARGET AREA 37

DEMOGRAPHICS 41

THE INGREDIENTS OF A NEW CHURCH 45

NATURAL PROCESS AND PERCEPTION 54

THE DISCIPLESHIP PHASE 64

OVERVIEW OF THE BUILDING PROCESS 72

THE BUILDING PROCESS 83

PASTORING A GROWING CHURCH 97

EFFECTIVE EVANGELISM TODAY 103

FOREWORD BY STEVE NICHOLSON

Steve Nicholson has generated a number of successful church plants from his base church in Evanston, Illinois and is also regarded as a leading teacher on church planting in the Vineyard USA. He is therefore qualified to look back on John Wimber's teaching with the wisdom of historical hindsight. Here is what he says.

1. In the early days with Wimber hundreds of leaders decided to plant churches. They had little training, very little support, no coaching in most cases and yet they went. Many moved to new cities in order to plant churches. Why? It was not because of the motivations talks so much as it was simply a result of a powerful experience of being called by the Holy Spirit. It seems to me that when the Spirit is moving in power He "ambushes" people and calls them into ministry. When that's not happening, church planting declines.

    I had already planted when I met Wimber, but that's how so many of our church plants came about.

2. Wimber's list of different models of church planting and his description of what a church planter should look like is still pure gold. Thirty-five years of experience have only confirmed his wisdom on these points.

3. I think a lot of his material on evangelism is still good as well, though often untried. It's definitely worth some serious study.

4. His stuff on demographics and the demography of the cities is out of date. His description is more accurate to 1970 reality but not to 2020 reality. The cities have changed dramatically in 50 years, in particular with the rise of a professional class taking over the central cities.

5. In his model for how to build a church plant John uses what I would call an inside-out model. In this model you begin with

evangelism, then add small groups, then eventually a Sunday meeting. Our experience was that while this worked well for some planters, for others it didn't work as well. Those whose primary gifts were public speaking found that the inside-out model meant a lot of early time when their primary gifts were not used. So we added what I call an outside-in model where a crowd is gathered quickly and then the internal structure is built from within that crowd. Many of the more recent church planting books encourage this approach.

6. John has some good stuff on finding and developing leaders, but I think it is somewhat culturally bound. If one is in a multi-cultural context then a more nuanced version would be necessary.

INTRODUCTION

John Wimber's passion for church planting either contributed to or lies at the historical genesis of the priority given to it in Vineyard, New Wine and HTB circles today. Through the entire course of his ministry, he modeled, inspired and taught it. This is his original teaching on the subject.

The specialist skills and vast experience he brought to the subject as a member of the Fuller School of World Missions provides us with a benchmark, or default document. Fundamentals are laid out here, which subsequent literature and story-telling can enlarge and develop. Our leaders should at least have imbibed this essential beginning.

While John Wimber is the original teacher and thinker, the grammar of the text is mine, as editor. Hence the title, "A resume" by Derek Morphew. While the excellence of the course derives from Wimber's lectures, any shortcomings will be due to the editorial process. The reader should be aware of how this course has been generated. There are various sets of taped lectures John gave, mostly early on in his ministry, and there are the Vineyard Bible Institute (of Anaheim) copyright tapes and course notes of 1997. Many of these lectures overlap. Together they provide a fairly comprehensive set of his teachings.

However, those who know how John operated will understand the shortcomings in any attempt to document his work. He usually had a research assistant, or a few, who wrote up the actual course material. They would shape and reshape it as he directed. There would normally be a booklet with a teaching outline prefaced by a few written paragraphs, as is the case here. When he came to teach live, he would follow his notes rather loosely, sometimes rushing through a section by simply reading out the headings aloud, at other times pausing on just one point and launching himself into extended storytelling or new material. The result is that some parts of the original outline have almost no comment, while other parts require new headings to be inserted.

INTRODUCTION

Further, John was usually in the habit of teaching with someone alongside. Some of the material was taught by Bob Fulton, later international coordinator of the Association of Vineyard churches, and his insights, also reflecting vast experience, also appear in those sections.

Creating a text that reads grammatically from a frequently passionate and animated John Wimber is not easy. This text is therefore not Wimber word for word. It is rather like a paraphrase of his words. Sometimes, when he has not commented on a section, there is some creative editorial insertion. It would have been too cumbersome to use quotes where we have his actual words, so original teacher, co-teacher and editor are merged. However, if instead of trying to reflect the thought of John or Bob, I have introduced post-dated information, this is reflected in footnotes. Any deficiency in the final result is therefore my responsibility, rather than Bob Fulton or John Wimber.

The original text has the following introductory remarks.

> Church planting and Kingdom theology have been at the heart of the Vineyard movement since its inception. Now, twenty years later, the Vineyard is raising a new generation of churches. In this course John shares his vision for expanding the Kingdom through planting new churches. He gives biblical, theological and practical reasons for planting new churches. He draws on his rich experience of raising up new leaders and planting new churches to envision a new generation of church planters.

> John Wimber is the pastor emeritus of the Vineyard, Anaheim, and the International Director of the Association of Vineyard Churches. Under his leadership, the church grew from a small home prayer meeting to over 5,000 members with an Association of more than 500 sister congregations around the world. The vision of AVC is to plant another 1,000 or more new churches by the year 2000.

Derek Morphew,
Ghost writer/producer, January 2020.

WHY PLANT NEW CHURCHES?

Today I will be introducing some general concepts on missiology as it relates to the planting of churches. I will be asking why we require new churches. Many of my remarks are based on a shared experience with my colleagues at Fuller. I worked for a number of years as a consultant to a number of church planting agencies in the Home Missions Department at Fuller and/or Church Planting Departments in various denominations. During a period of about six years I helped plant and/or strategize the planting of eight hundred churches.

All big churches were once small churches and there's nothing that grows like a new church. Trying to encourage the growth of an existing church is much more difficult than starting out fresh. There are many advantages and many difficulties in church planting, but if we are to reach this generation for Christ, it will have to be through new churches. We will not do it with the existing churches, regardless of how much renewal occurs. We not only need to renew the existing churches, but we need to plant thousands upon thousands of new churches.

NEW CHURCHES ARE NECESSARY FOR EFFECTIVE EVANGELISM

Empirical reasons for church planting

1. New churches are more efficient in evangelizing. The majority of the people who attend Protestant churches (53–54%) are not Christians, and they have been attending for 10 years or more. America is a 'nation of nomi nals' with 'believers who don't belong.' 82% of Americans say they are Christians, but only 37% go to church in a given week, down 5 years in a row to the lowest in a decade. Every year over 1 million people who die in America do not know Jesus Christ as Savior and Lord. This means that nominal Christians are in as much danger of eternal loss as unchurched non-Christians. In addition, the churches they attend

WHY PLANT NEW CHURCHES?

out of tradition are not likely to evangelize them. In contrast, new churches grow through winning new members. In this process the issues of conversion and discipleship are confronted. Evangelism is therefore inherent in new churches. Even when they grow from transfer growth, the process of internship normally involves a change from nominal, traditional faith to personal, saving faith.

2. If there are millions of nominal Christians still to be evangelized, there are also millions who have no relation to the church at all. According to Barna, 70% of the 265 million US population, or 185 million are non-Christians (nominal and unchurched). If these non-Christians were a nation, it would be the 5th largest nation on earth.

Church Planting and Urban Mission

There is a great need in urban areas in America today. 85% of all Americans now live in great cities. The Garden Grove Anaheim, our Santa Ana area has become a megapolis. The people who have moved into such areas are in a state of flux. They have left their roots, their background, their churches and their identity. Of the eleven and a half million people that live here in Southern California probably something less than 18–20% have any kind of real in-depth relationship with God. We have an incredible mission field all about us. This movement into urban areas has been going on now for some 50 years, all over the United States and all over the world. So, we must recognize if we are to win this generation for Christ, we are going to have to do it in the midst of the smog, on the sidewalks and in the streets, where the crime is. We are going to have to do it in the cities. That's where the people are. It is unfortunate that God did not die for clean air and pretty scenery. He died for people! We have got to go where the people are.

The cities today are unchurched. The more you get into the inner urban areas the more unchurched it becomes. One can view large cities as a series of concentric circles, from the inner city to the out fringe. As you move towards the center so plurality and poverty becomes the name of the game. Right in the midst of highest high rises are the poor. The racial plurality and transitory population is much more evident here.

If you are going to win the inner cities of America, you are going to have to be able to do it in multiple languages. There are 72 different languages between here and Los Angeles. If we are going to win the people in Southern California, we are going to have to preach the gospel in 72 different languages! We've got a job to do and it is complex.

The inner urban area is the rotten core of the city. Alongside incredible wealth we have this incredible poverty. Not only economic poverty, but poverty of soul, body and mind. To do the job we must move from the outer fringe inward, but most of the resources are going to come from the suburbs, or outer fringe, where there is more wealth. We have to generate resources so that we can move into the great cities. Our church started out at the Canyon. Now we have moved to the edge of the inner urban area of Orange County. We have done this intentionally. We prayed about it, we looked for a place, we roamed these streets for two years looking for a place and God finally opened this one up to us.

We need new churches on old ground and on new ground. The new ground is where the cities are sprawling outwards. The old ground is the inner city, the urban areas where the densest population is. People move either out or in because of economic reasons. Young couples may live way out or way into the city. You cannot live in suburbia any longer, not in Southern California, unless you are living on a previous generation's money. Either you are way out in the new developments, where you can still get a $55 000 to $75 000 dollar house, or you find a $75 000 shack in the inner urban area. We must recognize that we have to plant new churches on old ground as well as new churches on new ground to reach this generation. We have to do this geographically and demographically.

We must reach the lost sheep that have left the church. Most of us are nominal Christians, or second-generation church dropouts. Your parents went to a church and you dropped out some time in your teens. Then God drew you back at a later point. That is where most of the people come from that are being evangelized today.

The calling on the Vineyard

There is a correlation here with Paul's evangelistic ministry. He won the people that were on the periphery of the Synagogue. Similarly, most of our converts are coming from the periphery of church life, second-generation dropouts. So, we must plant new churches to reach the believers who do not belong. Gallop has said that there are 35 million believers who do not belong. They believe the Bible is the Word of God and they believe Jesus Christ is the Son of God, but they would not go to any church they now know of. They do not trust the church. However, the Vineyard is a very viable option for them. There are many reasons for this. We have designed our church to reach the medium age of the community. The church style, lifestyle, dress, model, have all been designed for the 'baby boom' generation. Look around you, at the medium age of all of you who are seated here.

You could not easily pastor a denominational church, unless you started one. Perhaps you could be an associate pastor. The medium age in the denominational church is 44 years of age. People over 44 are not going to take your counsel when you are 34, or 29. For the first five years of its existence the medium age of our church was 19. Now it's up to 23. The medium age of the Vineyard movement as far as I can tell is about 23. That is where I want to keep it, as a young people's church. Our calling, I think, is to reach the believers that do not belong. There are hundreds of thousands of them all about us. While they would not go to any church they now know of, once they see us, they are going to say, 'Oh, that's where I can go.' I don't have to dress up. I don't have to be different. I don't have to put on religious tones and learn how to speak a strange language. I don't have to sing songs that are not relevant. I can be actively involved in the church and I don't have to be a spectator, because the church is designed for the kind of dynamics that are with young people.

In Acts, text after text will show that evangelism leads to church planting. First comes evangelism, the penetration of the community with signs and wonders. Then as a result, the church comes into existence. Our church is experiencing spiraling growth at the moment.

Paul was an urban church planter. He bypassed the rural areas and the small communities. As far as I know, he didn't stop to witness to them. He went directly to the large urban area. Most of us have false perceptions of communities like Ephesus. It was not a sleepy little village, not on your life! The smallest of the cities Paul reached was 500,000 in size. Our calling is to model on Paul's strategy, to reach the great metropolises of the world. Once you have established major churches there then you can move out from there. One church, Ephesus probably planted in excess of 400 churches in Asia Minor. Ephesus was probably over 50,000 strong at its peak. They were not small churches by any means. Out of Ephesus came this incredible wave of young people, praying by example, precepts and model to go out and evangelize, heal the sick, cast out devils, preach the Gospel, train others, and multiply through discipleship. This was the secondary wave. The first wave was to reach the urban areas. There can be exceptions, if God really tells you to go to the second field first, but examine your guidance carefully. If you go fishing you want to go where the fish are, not where the shade is, with a nice picnic spot.

New churches have a fresh vitality

New churches adopt new models, new lifestyles, and new habits. If you go to an existing church, you have to re-direct it. It is like trying to get people to pay again for yesterday's lunch. If they have been in the church for a while and there was no costly commitment or discipleship required, that is what they expect. There wasn't any real involvement. All they had to do for church membership was to stand and give once or twice a year. It bugs them when you come along and say, 'Look now I want you to be in a small group, I want you to start training, I want you to learn how to cast out devils, I want you to heal the sick. I want you to help me go out and witness.' They'll say, 'Wait a minute, I don't want to do that, I like church the way it was'.

Therefore, if we want to train people effectively, we have to start new churches. To quote Peter Wagner, 'It is easier to have babies that to raise the dead.' New churches grow better than old churches. New churches are absolutely essential, if we are to do the job. They stimulate other churches in the area by bringing new life.

A common problem with church planters is other churches in the area will draw them into their agenda, because we care for and want to share with other churches. Young church planters get almost sucked into watching the other churches. But after having to earn a living, take care of their family, keep reasonably clean and start their own church they have no energy left to go out and do several hours for other churches. So, you have to prioritize your time. You first have to plant the church. Then when it has the resources you can give to others. First plant a few trees, get some harvest off it, and then you can share the apples. But if you share it too soon, you're just going to share the apple trees themselves.

During the foundational period everybody is down on the ground floor and operating from rudimentary basic discipleship. Everybody is learning to do the same thing, to pray, to share, to walk with others, to worship, to heal, to cast out demons, to study the word. There are about 15 basic practices that the community is learning at the same time. Maybe the pastor is half a page ahead of the others. Maybe, on some things, he is two pages behind. He is learning too. Everybody is learning basic lifestyle practices. This facilitates the development of new leaders, since everyone is starting together.

Because of the prevalence of Greek educational philosophy in our culture we tend to confuse professionalism with ministry. I have been in the ministry for 20 years. I was not ordained until 7 years after I was saved. I haven't always drawn a paycheck, but I have been 'in the ministry' from the beginning, no matter how I earned my living. The night I was saved I went into the ministry. I began witnessing and sharing with people the very next day. That night I went home and woke up my son and told him about Jesus. I started the same night and I have been doing it ever since! I am going to do it however I earn my living. I am going to share Christ with people, to confront them, bug them, tell them that they're going to hell without Jesus, but with Jesus they don't have to. I am going to keep bugging them until I get them saved. Then I am going to bug them until they go with me and we bug others. I am going to do that whether I earn my living selling shoes, or insurance, or whatever. I have done it for long periods of time. I am going to pray for the sick, study the Word and to worship God. These basics are my life. Until you come to that point, until you have committed yourself to being a disciple, you cannot disciple others. You have to be a disciple to make disciples. Somebody has to gather disciples. You have to get the first one to make the second. I have been doing it for 20 years and I'm getting pretty good at some of it. There is still a lot I am not as good at as I want to be. But I am going to do it, and do it, and do it, and do it and do it some more. I am going do it whether I fail, whether people turn on me, or whether I succeed.

BIBLICAL REASONS FOR CHURCH PLANTING

On every occasion where there was a move of the Spirit of God it resulted in people being brought into the church. A key text is Acts 2:42–47.

> They devoted themselves to the apostles' teaching and to the fellowship, to the breaking of bread and to prayer. Everyone was filled with awe, and many wonders and miraculous signs were done by the apostles. All the believers were together and had everything in common. Selling their possessions and goods, they gave to anyone as he had need. Every day they continued to meet together in the temple courts. They broke bread in their homes and ate

together with glad and sincere hearts, praising God and enjoying the favor of all the people. And the Lord added to their number daily those who were being saved.

This is one of the most comprehensive statements in the Book of Acts concerning the nature and the activity of the church. The description of rapid growth is something we can relate to in our context. We've had seasons here in this church where we've seen hundreds of people saved over a period of time. In recent months we baptized almost 300 new converts.

Note, those who were added to their numbers were added to the church, not necessarily to the disciples. The job's not over if you just catch them. You've got to clean them. You've got to bring them into the church! That's the goal. It's discipleship. The characteristics of the New Testament Churches are clear:

- they study,
- they fellowship,
- they break bread and
- they pray.

My wife and I have stood in our living room many times since the formation of this church began. We have said to each other, 'whether anyone else does, we are going to fellowship, to teach the word, to break bread and to pray.' The bottom line is that you have to take on the lifestyle you want to propagate, otherwise what you multiply is something that is inconsistent or incomplete. Whatever you are is what your people will be.

'Every day they continued to meet together in the Temple court.' How often? Every day. Notice the contagious nature of fellowship? They had to be together, to support, encourage, interact and build intimacy, relationship and accountability. 'The Lord added to their numbers daily, those who were being saved.' The goal of the event was church planting, anything less than that is incomplete.

The other vital text, Acts 1:8, provides us with an 'evangelistic axis.'

> But you will receive power when the Holy Spirit comes on you; and you will be my witnesses in Jerusalem, and in all Judea and Samaria, and to the ends of the earth.

This text can be unpacked in various ways. In the following analysis we will examine the spread of both evangelism and church planting. When they received this word from Jesus, they were gathered in Jerusalem. Wherever we are is now our 'Jerusalem', our mission base. From that point their ministry grew in ever widening circles.

The book of Acts gives prominence to the spreading of the word of God, or what Michael Green called the 'gossiping of the gospel' (Acts 4:29,31; 6:2,4,7; 8:4,14,25; 11:1; 12:24; 13:5,7,15,44,46,48,49; 14:25; 15:27,35,36; 16:6,32; 17:13; 18:11; 19:10, 20; 20:32).

We will examine the broad pattern of evangelism and church planting and then break it down into its parts.

Evangelistic Axis			
Web relationships	Near neighbors	Far neighbors	World
E–0	E–1	E–2	E–3
	CP–1	CP–2	CP–3
Jerusalem	**Judea**	**Samaria**	**Antioch/Rome**
Antioch	Syria		Antioch
Thessalonica	Macedonia		Ephesus
Ephesus	All in Asia		Thessalonica
			Rome

Notice in the middle row that the word of Jesus in Acts 1:8 is the basis of the history that follows. As is commonly noted, the formula provided in 1:8 corresponds to the structure of Acts that follows.

The left-hand column describes what occurred within the mission base churches. Here people were not having to move out geographically but sharing with their own community. There was no 'outreach' in evangelism, so we call this E–0. This does not mean that one does not spread the word. It just means we do not have to go anywhere to do so.

In the next column we have the first relationship with the base (left column). To those in Jerusalem Judea was their province. Wherever you are in a city, there will be villages and towns around you. They are normally populated by people like you. You have to make a modest geographical journey to reach them, but you do not have to cross any cultural barriers. For those in Antioch, their province was Syria, for those in Thessalonica, it was the province of Macedonia, for those in Ephesus, the province of Asia. It was the practice of the early church to move from metropolitan base to the next. This is the how the narrative of Acts progresses. These city bases became the point from which evangelism and church planting moved into the provinces.

The third column shows the gospel breaking its first cultural barrier. The Samaritans were Hebrews, but not of pure ancestry. They worshiped Yahweh, but from Mount Gerazim, not Jerusalem. For each of us in the world today, there will be a culture near to us, yet requiring some cross-cultural communication. These are our far-neighbors, neighbors because they are close to our culture and not too far geographically, 'far' because we have to cross a cultural barrier.

The right column follows the narrative of the third part of Acts, with the various Pauline missionary journeys. It tells the story of the gospel spreading from Antioch to Rome. It shows how they moved from base to base.

The two E and CP rows above show how the pattern with evangelism corresponds to the pattern with church planting.

The following table begins to work out this analysis in the case of the church at Jerusalem.

		Evangelism from Jerusalem	
Axis	Geographical	Text	Relation to Base/*Text reference*/Description
E-0	Jerusalem		*Web Relationships*
		2:47	*… enjoying the favor of all the people. And the Lord added to their number daily those who were being saved.*
		4:4	*But many who heard the message believed, and the number of men grew to about five thousand.*
		5:14	*Nevertheless, more and more men and women believed in the Lord and were added to their number.*
		6:1	*In those days when the number of disciples was increasing …*
		6:7	*So the word of God spread. The number of disciples in Jerusalem increased rapidly, and a large number of priests became obedient to the faith.*
		12:24	*But the word of God continued to increase and spread.*
E-1	Judea		*Near neighbors*

		8:1	On that day a great persecution broke out against the church at Jerusalem, and all except the apostles were scattered throughout Judea and Samaria.
E-2	*Samaria*		**Far neighbors**
		8:1	...were scattered throughout Judea and Samaria.
		8:5–24	Evangelism in the city of Samaria
		8:25	Evangelism in other villages in the Province of Samaria.
E-3	*Ends of earth*		**The world**
		2:9–11	Pentecost and the various language groups
		8:4	Evangelism at Antioch
		11:19–20	Evangelism at Antioch

The following table indicates the spread of church planting.

Church Planting from Jerusalem			
Axis	Geographical	Text	Relation to base/text reference/description
CP–1	*Judea*		**Near neighbors**
		9:31	The church throughout Judea
		1 Thess.2:14	Became imitators of God's churches in Judea
		Gal.1:22	Churches in Judea
CP–2	*Samaria*		**Far neighbors**
		9:31	The church throughout ... Samaria
		15:3	Sent with the edict from the Council of Jerusalem to the churches in Samaria
CP–3	*Ends of earth*	2:10	Tradition has it that the church at Rome was founded by those saved in Jerusalem at Pentecost.
		11:26	A church at Antioch resulted from evangelism

The point is in the comparison between these two tables. There is a direct relation between the spread of the word through evangelism and the planting of churches. The same broad sweep of geographical enlargement is used to describe the word going out and churches being planted. Wherever the word was spread, if we check later, we find churches there.

The two left columns follow the same geographical pattern. The right columns show evangelism occurring in the first chart, and the result, in churches planted, in the second chart.

Evangelism from Antioch			
Axis	Geographical	Text	Relation to Base/*Text reference*/Description
E–0		11:21,24	E–3 Evangelism from church at Jerusalem
E–2	*Syria*	15:41	*Paul chose Silas and left ... He went through Syria and Cilicia, strengthening the churches.*
E–3	*Ends of earth*	4:4	The world
		13:4	Cyprus
		13:13–14:26	Galatia
		16:11–14	Macedonia, including Thessalonica
		16:16–18:17	Achaia
		18:19; 19:1–41	Asia, including Ephesus

Church Planting from Antioch			
Axis	Geographical	Text	Relation to Base/*Text reference*/Description
CP–2	*Syria*	15:41	He went through Syria and Cilicia, strengthening the churches.
CP–3	*Ends of earth*		The world
		16.5	*So the churches were strengthened in the faith and grew daily in numbers.*
		14:23; Gal.1:2; 1 Cor.16:1	Planted churches in Galatia
		2 Cor.8:1 Phil.4:15	Planted churches in Macedonia: Philippians, Berea, Thessalonica
		2 Cor.2:1 Rom.16:1	Planted churches in Achaia—Corinth Cenchrea
		1 Cor.16:19 Rev.1:4	Planted churches in Asia

Once again, the comparison between the two tables shows the relationship between evangelism and church planting. In the first table are references to the spread of the Word, in the second are references to churches found in those areas.

	Evangelism from Thessalonica		
Axis	Geographical	Text	Relation to Base/*Text reference*/Description
E-1	*Macedonia*	1 Thess.1:8	*The Lord's message rang out from you not only* **in Macedonia** ...
E-2	*Achaia*	1 Thess.1:8	*The Lord's message rang out from you not only in ...* **Achaia**--*your faith in God has become known everywhere.*
E-3	*Beyond*	1 Thess.1:8	*The Lord's message rang out from you not only in Macedonia and Achaia--your faith in God has become known* everywhere.

The pattern is that churches spring up where the gospel is preached. Those in Macedonia, Achaia and beyond were reached by the Thessalonian Christians. We are not told of the churches they planted, but we can be sure they were planted.

	Evangelism from Ephesus		
Axis	Geographical	Text	Relation to Base/*Text reference*/Description
E-0	*Ephesus*		E-3 evangelism from Antioch
		19:1–7	Paul: The disciples of John the Baptist
		19:20	*In this way the word of the Lord spread widely and grew in power.*
E-1	*Asia*	19:9–10	*He took the disciples with him and had discussions daily in the lecture hall of Tyrannus. This went on for two years, so that all the Jews and Greeks who lived in the province of Asia heard the word of the Lord.*

We know that churches were planted from the church base in Ephesus. The letter to the Ephesians does not have 'at Ephesus' in the greeting in the most ancient manuscripts. From its content and who is addressed within, it is a circular letter written to a number of local churches, particularly up the Lycus valley from Ephesus. It is closely related to Colossians, which mentions the church at Laodicea (Colossians 4:6). The letters to the seven churches in Revelation 2–3 show a time when there were seven in the immediate area. John had been based in Ephesus, from where he was sent into exile on Patmos.

VINEYARD CHURCH PLANTING

Put simply, church planting is how we understand our mission. While we engage in all sorts of activities set out in our genetic code, the focus is church planting. It is what this family does! In 1983 the Anaheim Vineyard was the 7th to be added to the fledgling movement started by Kenn Gulliksen. With the entry of this church, led by John, the movement was restructured to reflect this emphasis, and rapidly grew to 25 churches. By 1996 there were 411 churches in the USA.

It was not long before church planting moved beyond the USA to include churches in other countries. The following graphs supply the details.[1]

AVC-USA Growth 1983-1996

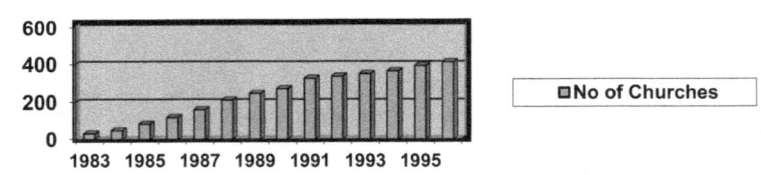

---

[1] These graphs are derived from the Vineyard Bible Institute course of 1997, *God's Heart for Expanding the Kingdom through Church Planting*. The first graph details only the USA statistics, from 1983 to 1996. The three graphs that follow reflect figures obtained from Bob Fulton, whose responsibility it was to work with Vineyard ministries outside of the USA. I hope to get updates on these graphs from Mark Fields, the one person best qualified to supply accurate statistics, when he has time to do so. Bob explained them at the time as follows:

> "The graphs reflect a detailed set of figures in an Excel file. The figures for 2001–2003 reflect the same source for the USA for 2000–2001 but this source has no figures for 2001–2003 for the other countries and no figures for the USA for 2003. Here I have calculated average figures for 2001 and 2002, based on parity of 600 each in 2003. This last bit or information for 2003 was gathered from Mark Fields. The second shows the total growth, giving one some idea of what to extrapolate into the future on the basis of a similar growth curve. The third shows the total number of countries where Vineyard churches have been planted, excluding the USA."

WHY PLANT NEW CHURCHES?

Number of Countries 1986-2000

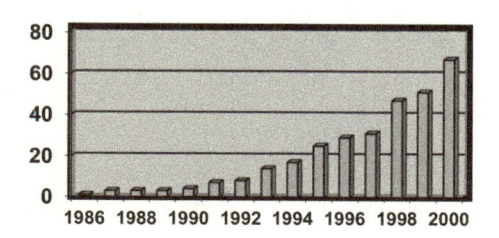

USA & Other Countries 1986-2003

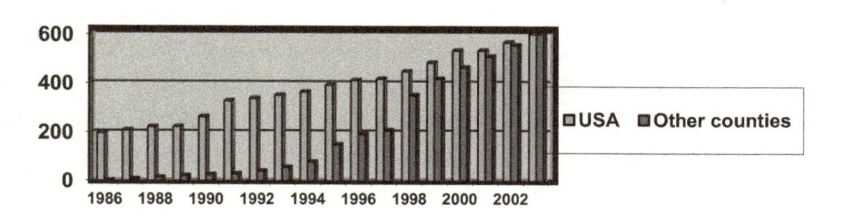

CHURCH PLANTING MODELS

MODALITY MODELS

1. Hiving off

In other literature this is often described as a mother-daughter church plant. It normally occurs when a growing number of people have been attending the mother church from some distance. Possibly a number of home groups have developed in the area. They begin to figure out that all the people added together would make a viable congregation. If a competent leader exists within the group, or is available from within the mother church, the viability increases. The mother church then sends out a group with a pastor for the new church. Groups 'hived-off' can vary in size but may be quite large (100 people).

2. Colonization

This is where the mother church sends a group of people to physically relocate to another area. The area will be too far away for the mother church to have any members there. Normally a smaller group will be involved (perhaps 10–20). While the first model occurs through natural growth, this method is more intentional and requires more initiative. Those involved will require a greater sense of calling.

3. Adoption

A group has come into being without the involvement of the mother church. However, they conclude that they need assistance from the mother church and invite its participation. Sometimes the mother church will supply a leader lacking in the emerging group. Alternatively, the group may simply be nurtured from the mother church.

4. Accidental parenthood

This occurs through a 'split' of some kind. While all splits are painful, and probably sinful, the net result can be an extension of the Kingdom and the birth of a new church. God can somehow bless all parties involved.

5. The satellite model

In this model the 'daughter' churches take longer to 'leave home.' The mother church may be structured as a multiple-congregational church, or it may develop a number of sub-structures on its periphery, where a large celebration type meeting has various smaller gatherings scattered around it. The pastors of the satellite congregations will be associates of the mother church. Sometimes finances are centralized. Sometimes they are broken into various sub-accounts. As time goes on some congregations further towards the periphery may become autonomous. In this model things generally occur in a more evolutionary manner, creating less stress for the mother church.

6. Multi-congregational churches

A common form of this model is where a number of different ethnic or language groups use the same building. Alternatively, a cluster of congregations in a city will form a type of 'federal' structure. Some functions will be given to the 'federal' body (offices, finances, training, large gatherings), while other functions will be the responsibility of each congregation (home groups, community services). Some will gather separately on a weekly basis and then 'celebrate' once a month or once every six weeks. In other settings they will meet separately on Sunday mornings and together on Sunday evenings, or vice versa.

7. Multiple campus model

A common form of this model is where a Sunday morning meeting serves a typical adult congregation, with families, kids ministry etc., and a Sunday night gathering reaches young adults (18–30 years old). The two meetings will not occur at the same venue (the young adults could meet on or near a campus), but the church will be one in its leadership, offices, finances etc. This model can then be extended to include various preaching points in the same city.

While modality models focus on the people groups involved, sodality models focus more on the agencies that do the planting.

SODALITY MODELS

1. The mission team

A group of churches from the same movement or denomination in a city or region can agree to a common vision in church planting and mission. A group of people, usually with a sense of calling, and perhaps after some training, can be gathered from such a group of churches and sent to start a new church in a new area. This can occur on a short or long-distance basis. If the team can travel to and from the mission area by car, perhaps over weekends, the mission is less demanding. Alternatively, such teams can service church plants in other countries, and plan a number of mission trips a year. This model has been adopted where various churches partner between countries with greater resources and countries with a scarcity of resources.

2. The catalytic church planter

The catalytic church planter is a uniquely gifted individual or couple who move into a new area, gather people, start a church, and then invite a 'settler' type pastor to take over, at which point they move on to start another one. They will normally leave within one or two years. Some, in certain societies where evangelism is rapid, will move on after six to eight weeks.

3. The founding pastor

The founding pastor begins like the catalytic church planter but does not move on. He stays there to build up the church and settle.

THE CHURCH PLANTERS PROFILE

We will now focus on the leader, the one who catalyzes growth. Not everybody is supposed to be that person. With church planting teams, or apostolic church planting teams, not everybody on the team plays the catalytic role. Some can work as support people in teams that start churches. Our focus here is on the leading role in such a team.

CRITERIA

Able to gather people

To be a successful catalytic church planter you have to be able to gather people. If you are not able to gather people, get somebody else who can. The kind of person who can gather people is the type who tended to put the parties together at High School, who put the ball games together. You know how to get the people to come: 'You bring this, and you bring that.'

Self-starters who can endure loneliness

Church planters have to be able to endure loneliness and keep on going. So often church planters are desperate and just need fellowship. We need someone to call us once in a while, talk to us, write us a letter, or come by and see us, because we are desperate and lonely. It's all 'give' the first couple of years. There is very little coming back at you. It is a little like moving out to Arizona and buying 20 acres to start planting corn. From the time that you buy the land, till the sod and put corn in the ground, it is a long time before you have corn on the cob, especially if you have a few crop failures. If there is one thing you can be confident about in starting churches is that you are going to have some crop failures. People you are really committed to are not going to be committed to you. Groups you started will go to other churches. People will turn away from you and turn you down.

This will hurt. But it will identify you with the suffering of Jesus. He also got disappointed with his disciples. But He loved them anyway. That is the name of the game. The basic unit that keeps you going is you and Him: He and you and you and Him, and him and her, if you have got a 'her' or a 'him.' You and Him and him and her and them, if you have got some of 'them.' This is the way it works.

Church planters need to have no illusions. It really must be a supernatural enterprise. It really does require God's anointing for this thing to work, but it does work, it does happen. All the big churches had to start right there. Somewhere somebody got lonely, but somebody did it. To come to that commitment requires you to be a self-starter. Loneliness is a reality that is native to the activity of leaving. It's just the way it is.

Adaptable and pragmatic

You must be adaptable and you must be pragmatic in your adaptability. Some people are so enamored with fishing that they would rather cast the reel than catch fish. I don't like fishing. I like ketching. It took me ten minutes when I was 11 years old with my grandpa to find out that I don't like fishing. I like bringing those fish in.

I don't like playing church. There's nothing about it that I like. I like winning souls, bringing people into the Kingdom, discipling them, training them, sending them out. I like that. I don't like that other stuff. I just don't have any energy for that other stuff. I can't stay with it.

Most of what we call the work of the church today is like playing basketball without hoops or balls. This morning I went through about 25 letters. At least ten of them were from organizations that had no ball and no hoops. 'Give me your money and give me your leadership.' That is what they were asking for, after you read the letter. 'Here's my prayer letter, here's what I'm doing,' but no basketball and no hoops.

We are encouraging you to have a hoop and a ball. When you are through it is called a church. It's not street evangelism per se, it's not going to the beach for the weekend and witnessing to a few lost souls, it's not sending Bibles to China, it's not doing 500 other things, that are profitable and good. It is about getting people churched! How far you have progressed in building a community is a measurable goal. Once a community exists, which is revealing God's love in the world, redeeming the community, redeeming the family, building a place of restoration in the midst of our broken world, then you have a church. It is redeeming the drug addict, the homosexual and the lesbian, bringing the family into relationship with one another and keeping them together. It is the work of God in the community, it is measurable, it has hoops and it has a ball!

You can tell when you're scoring. With almost all the ministries that are out there today, you can't tell when you're scoring. It's enough to have the illusion of scoring. In sales we called it smelling the sizzle, like when you can smell your neighbor's steak cooking on the barbecue. 'Oh, doesn't that smell good. We are going to get 3000 people together. This is a great project. All we need is some of your people and some of your money.' I say 'pass'. We want to give our energy where people are planting churches because there is the hoop. I can look at the scorecard. It only takes me a couple of minutes. How many people have you gathered into community?

He is a self-starter, he is adaptable, and he is pragmatic. Whatever works is what I keep doing, what doesn't work I quit. Never be too committed to any particular program or method. There is no one method of evangelism. Currently kinship groups are helpful and important in the church. But when they cease to be effective, we will move on to something else. We will have some other kind of small group. I know we will always have small groups, but what they are called and what they do may evolve and evolve and evolve and evolve and evolve. I am not committed to a single program we have in our church. I am not interested in institutions and traditions. I am interested in facts. Are people being changed? Are groups forming? Does the church make a difference in the community?

Somebody called me the other day. He said, 'I heard you preached on such and such, is that the way the Vineyard preachers are going to preach from now on (disapproving tone)?' I said, 'I don't know about the rest of them, but that's where I'm at right now'. I am not interested in a style or form or approach or anything. I am interested in following after God. I am committed to go with God. If it isn't going with God, I'm out. I'm not trying to perpetuate anything. I'm not trying to build an organization. I'm not trying to build a denomination. I don't even want a personal ministry. I just want God. I joined up for God. Did you join up for God? Is that what you're after? Then you will be satisfied. I am after a relationship with the living God, but I am not after trying to build a movement. I am not trying to build a big church.

Faith and self-esteem

We call them possibility thinkers. It might surprise you to know that I watch Robert Schuler almost every week. I like Bob Schuler. He is a good friend of mine. He has been very kind and very loving towards me. I don't necessarily agree with all his theology, but I agree with men that influence other men to Christ. Bob Schuler influences men and women to Christ. Now he doesn't do it the way I would do it and he doesn't do all that I'd want him to do. He may be confused on some points theologically. I understand he doesn't preach sin properly. But I know this much. When he saw people being healed, he wept like a baby. When his daughter got filled with the Holy Ghost he fell on his knees and cried and hugged her.

I think church planters fall into one of two categories out of four:

1. Explorers
2. Pioneers
3. Homesteaders, or
4. Community planters.

They are either explorers or pioneers. They are not homesteaders or community planters. An explorer does not go on to stay. He goes to map the turf to find out what's there. Church planting fits somewhere between exploring and pioneering. A homesteader comes after somebody has established things. Many pastors of churches are not pioneers. More of them are homesteaders. Some church planters start churches and then move on. Some plant churches and settle down. Then there are those who come along after the church planter to establish the church. My point is, there is room for several different kinds of profiles: those that will go before, those who will come and stay, and those who will come after. My assumption is that most us are focused on going before.

A supportive family

You have to have a supportive family. Church planting takes incredible self-sacrifice. Some of you will have to postpone having children, some of you will have to take your children with you. Many things will have to become subordinate to your goal. It's a sacrifice to do this work. It's not for everybody. But someone is supposed to go do this. It is not something that you can just put on your family. You can't just say, 'now listen woman, if you're going to stay married to me, you've got to be wife to that sort of husband, this is the way it's going to be'. God should have spoken to both of you.

I have a friend that planted about six churches. When he got saved the Spirit of God had been dealing with him for a couple of years. He tried to run away from the Lord, so he moved to Montana. He was clearing some brush with a big tractor one day and the tractor tipped over and fell on him. He couldn't get out from under the tractor. Its full weight was settling on him and he could hear his ribs cracking one at a time. Finally he said 'alright God.' He knew that commitment to Christ was commitment to Christ's work. The Lord had made that clear to him in a revelation. So, he knew that he was not just becoming a nominal Christian. He didn't want to go into the ministry. He hated the idea. So, his ribs are getting broken one at a time, both legs were broken right above the kneecaps.

When he said 'alright Lord, I give in' the tractor quit falling. He was able to dig himself out after half an hour and crawl on his elbows, two miles back to the ranch house. As he got to the yard, his wife came running out. She had the grace of God on her, the Glory of God on her face! The Lord has visited her and spoken to her. While she was in the kitchen the Lord told her what he had done to her husband and why he had done it. He was calling them to start churches.

You think the Lord will treat somebody that rough? You bet! I know many guys that the Lord has threatened with their very lives. So, when he wants you to do something, you're well advised to say 'Yes'.

A leader

To be a leader of people he needs to be Spirit led. He needs to know where he's going and how to get there.

A leader is just someone who knows the next step. That's all a leader is. If somebody yells FIRE right now the person who knows how to get out of here will be the leader. It is just knowing the next step. You don't have to know every step, you don't have to know the whole thing, you just need to know the next step. To know the next step means you need to know how to listen to God. That is all he ever gives me, the next step. He never gives me clear pictures for the future. What he was stirring me about this week was just really a fragment of the whole. I never know all the steps. I just know the next step. But it behooves us to learn how to hear from God so that we at least get that.

For instance, God has been dealing with me constantly for nearly six months now on this issue of prayer. I find myself praying upwards of two and three hours a day now. Just praying almost constantly to the Lord and listening, really listening! I have never given that kind of time to devotional life before. I have never had the time or never been willing to spare the time. He just quit asking me and started making me do it. He is speaking to me more and more because I am spending more time with Him. He used to have to speak to others because I wasn't spending any time. He would speak to my wife. One time I asked him, 'how come you always talk to my wife when you want me to do something?' He said 'Well she hangs around and listens'. Isn't it terrible! Somebody wants to serve God, but he won't spend any time with Him, talking with him or listening. So, God, Praise His name, has been teaching me how to listen to Him.

Able to relate to the unchurched

They ought to be able to relate to the un-churched. I'm still more comfortable standing in a beer bar than I am in the average church. I really am, it is easier for me to stand and talk to people, better than it is in the average church. Religious people just tend to turn me off. I hate religion. I was at a meeting this week in Fort Worth. God bless them, they were singing the oldest 'Marching to Zion' songs. Finally, after about three days of it, it struck my spirit and I really went after them. I said, 'This is an abomination of the Lord, you're not marching to Zion, you're sitting on your rumps. There's not a person in this room that means that, you're singing it because it came out of a tradition when there were some marchers, but you couldn't march to save your life, at this point of your life.' Then the Lord confirmed it with power. Boy, He just swept that room and a deep repentance came over the people. I wasn't saying it to be a big shot or smart Alec, I was saying it because it struck my spirit. We sing all these songs we don't mean and pray all these prayers we don't have any commitment to.

Called

Most of us are saying 'yes Lord' one minute and 'no' for the next ten. It's time we started coming to grips with His Word and began doing what he called us to do. He called us to be obedient, didn't He? If you don't know you are called by God, then stay on your face before him until you do. Because if you don't know that God has called you, it will be a major chink in your armor. That will be the one thing the enemy will be able to access again and again. If you don't know your call, then go before God and become an animal. Scream and holler, sweat, beat the floor, read the Word, fast and pray and call out until you are hoarse and then listen until you can't listen anymore and then do it some more. Until God speaks to you!

He will speak to you. But if He hasn't spoken to you, you are wasting your time and you are always going to be a problem to everybody else that is called. You will, you will be a constant problem to them. So, go before God and see if you know who you are, and what you have been called to do. It is not safe to play with people who do not know. When things get hard, they will split. And things are going to get hard. I will say that again, things are always going to get hard. It is hard to do this work!

You see for me I have no option. If you know you are called, then there is a basic indissoluble dynamic in your inner man. You know what you're for. If you know what you're for, it just makes everything easy.

I remember one time I was working with Pete Wagner and we had been teaching for probably three weeks in a row 8–10 hours a day in these big conferences and we were just exhausted. We got up one morning and we only had about 3 hours because of plane rides and everything. We were jet-lagged and all and I looked at him and he looked at me and grinned and said, 'aren't you glad you know what you're for?' He said, 'I wouldn't work this hard for anybody, or any money or anything I know of, except Him.' And we just cried because that's the truth. You had better know what you are for. There is only one person that can answer that issue for you. Your wife can't answer that issue, your friends can't answer that issue, God has to answer that issue.

The ability to recognize and release leaders

Right from the start, know that all of you are going to fail at this. I have released many people that have floundered and failed. It has been terrible for them, really terrible! I can close my eyes and I can picture couples that are no longer married because I made the mistake of releasing them. It cost them their marriage. So, I don't say this lightly. One of the reasons I am keen to obey the biblical injunction to 'not lay hands on any man suddenly' is because I have laid hands quickly on men and watched what happened to them as a result. I am much slower these days to lay hands on people. People come and say, 'I was in the church 5 years and I was ahead of that guy,' as if we ought to have some sort of priority of tenure or something. I just bless them. I say I just talked to God and He said, 'You know it's mine to send.' It's not my role, but His. You're chomping at the bit, but you're talking to the wrong person. Go talk to Him. If He wants you to go, He will send you. In the meantime, learn the basics, occupy till He comes. Some say, 'Oh I know basics, I can do everything.' My reply is, 'Well if you can why isn't He sending you?' Wait on the Lord.

This is not a man-made operation. We are not in the tough waters yet. At the moment we are going to America. Wait until He sends us to some of the other countries of the world. You think it is tough to go without coffee 3 days a week, how will you do in harsher environments?

The ability to recognize and release leaders is something you will all have difficulty with. I have released all kinds of people who have been hurt and harmed. I have also released some that have had incredible success. Most of the ones that have had success are the ones you see. The others have disappeared. They are in piles and heaps all over the county. I see them from time to time and they won't even look me in the eye, because I have hurt them so dreadfully! They are disappointed in themselves, they are disappointed in God and they are disappointed in me and they hate me for it. And I cry for them. I plead their case before God. So, do not be so quick to release people just because they are pressing you and say they are ready. They think they are ready, and you want to get them out of your hair, so you say, 'well go ahead'. I've got them all over the place. We have had our successes, but believe me, we have also had our failures, everywhere. I can hardly go any place without running into one or two.

By last autumn I had personally prayed for somewhere between 7 and 10,000 people in this country to receive Christ. I am not talking about public meetings, but about one on one. I have been here a long time. I have been an active Christian for 20 years. I have taught Bible Studies in almost every kind of neighborhood. I have started hundreds and hundreds of small groups. I have laid hands on hundreds of men. I didn't know how easily the enemy could swallow them up. I thought it was easy, because it was easy for me. So, if you ask me to lay hands on you and I just sort of give you a funny look, the reason is because I don't trust these hands to do that anymore. I am afraid of what may happen to you. That is why I am hesitating. It is not that I see anything bad or negative in you, or because I have made some sort of judgment on your life. I am scared to let people go, unless God speaks. But when I know God has spoken, then I am ruthless. 'Get out of here, go, I don't want you, go anywhere. God wants you to go.' You see the difference?

It is very helpful to start out with some church people, some nucleus that have some basic understanding of what you are doing and what you are all about. That can be a detriment when you are going out a long distance. The people will begin looking back over their shoulders, saying, 'we didn't do it that way in Anaheim.' They were ready to start a new church, but they were not ready to start a new life and learn new things. When you go out to start a church some people can be a blessing and curse at the same time. They can help you at first and then become a hindrance later on, because they will try to hold you to church life as they knew it, instead of letting God form and reform something new. Watch out for that, it is very, very common when you are starting a new work. People must let God form a new thing, let Him breathe life into a new body, with new characteristics and new dynamics.

If there is anything I want you to hold to, it is that life changes, forms and reforms constantly. I am not interested in trying to perpetuate a model. All I want is for us to be biblical. You do need to have a philosophy of ministry. You must have a concept of what kind of church are you planting, what is it that you are trying to build? An architect draws a plan in advance, he sees it in his mind's eye.

When our church started, I had a picture of what I wanted. I knew where we were going. I had an instinct for it. I had training, I had research, and I had revelation for it. God began showing me early on. I did not see the whole picture. I didn't know the full plan. I didn't even know the priorities.

God had already started with worship before I got involved. He spoke to me and said 'that's my foundation here, worship.' It is teaching people how to worship God, learning how to love Him with all their heart and soul—that's our highest single priority as a fellowship.

Our second priority is to focus on building fellowship groups. I really don't care what kind, prayer groups, bible study groups, evangelism groups, mission groups, or fellowship groups. 'Let's go to Mexico twice a month to minister down there'. That is a fellowship group, a place where people can interact and be intimate and care for one another and do things together, where they can know and be known, where they can be intimate and accountable. Fellowship!

God said that was to be the second priority in our church. It may not be the second one in your church. I am sure it will be in there somewhere, because it is the bible's pattern, but it will not necessarily be in that order in every church. I know churches right now that are really struggling in the area of worship. They don't even have a worship leader. I am not trying to make you a Vineyard. I am trying to help you to learn how to work with God in your community. Maybe your first priority is teaching the Word.

Maybe your first priority is fellowship, and maybe your first priority is evangelism. Because that is what God wants done there. We are trying to focus on how to get in contact with God, hearing from Him and moving with Him. In our church He spoke to us about worship and birthed it. These things are not just taken out of a book or absorbed some place. They are birthed. There is a gestation period. Then when it comes forth it becomes the pattern of the church. They must to be birthed among us, not adopted. We will always worship, have fellowship in small groups, and we will always train and disciple people. We will always minister out in the communities. These things have been birthed in us. They are always going to be part of our pattern.

You need to look at what has been birthed in you as an individual or a couple, then look at what has been birthed in the group. Pray and ask, 'Lord show me what is it we are already'? What am I going to be doing even if the church does not happen? Am I going to worship the Lord? Am I going to study his Word, am I going to witness to people, am I going to pray for the sick? If you can say yes, I am going to do those four things and maybe 10 others, then those things are already birthed in you. That is what you are. You are going to do that, whether you are in this church or in that church or whether you're a milkman or a postman or a doctor. Whatever your occupation you're going to do those things. Then you can know that they are really birthed in you.

If you have got to have a platform and a title and a place in order to do those things, then they are not birthed in you. It is like in the genetic make-up of your children. It comes out of genes. What your church is going to be is what is already in you now. I was visiting a church a few months ago. It is not technically a church as they don't meet on Sundays, but it is a fellowship of people. There are about 20 of them. The whole time I was talking to the leader he was apologizing for the size of the group. When I got to the meeting in his house the Spirit of the Lord was there, like a fragrance in the room—just the presence of God. The people worshipped beautifully. I mean they didn't all sing in tune, and the piano player was playing a poor piano and there were lots of technical problems. But the Spirit of God was there because their hearts were so pure. The fellowship was beautiful. He talked with eloquence and simplicity. While I was being blessed he was apologizing for the size of his church and wanted me to teach. Half kidding I said, 'you jerk, you don't know what you've got here. God in heaven is visiting you and ministering to you and through you and you're apologizing. There are men in big buildings all over this place who don't have what you have. You've got the resources of heaven working.' He started grinning and said, 'do I?' I said 'Yeh man, I'm not kidding you, this is what it's all about.'

It doesn't matter if its 20 or 200. If you've got that you've got everything. It's all there. There is no hurry to add to the numbers if there is nothing there to begin with. How many do you want to gather if they are unhappy, frustrated, angry, full of malice and bitterness and junk? I don't want any. There are already enough of those kind of churches, they're all around us. We want people that are harmonizing with God and one another and that are tuned and resonating to His presence, and operating in the context of the Kingdom. So, don't be in a hurry. Some try to develop a timetable. Then they are frustrated because after 6 months they have achieved so little of their timetable. May God bless them, but they missed the point. Take your time, smell the roses. Walk with Jesus. Enjoy and savor his presence.

If you are doing some things fundamentally wrong, then you need help. You could be basking in His favor, enjoying all those things and just not meeting enough people. There is no way your church can multiply. But the church must come out from some sort of an embryonic nucleus group just enjoying and savoring the Lord. If you have that, the church will grow. It will be a lovely garden with His presence. However, if you do not have that, then you don't need to grow. Quality is the way. There is no hurry to get quantity if you are not growing from a base of quality. Do not bypass the life in order to get the numbers. Keep yourself focused on Him and walking with Him.

We have various courses on our values and philosophy of ministry, but the key in my mind is that you find what is important to you. Years ago I preached a series on the church I would join. It wasn't a very good series, but it really met my need because it said what I wanted our church to be like. It was a gathering point for people because they realized that if that is the one I wanted to be in, then that is probably the one I was going to have eventually. The Lord used that on me some years ago. I was walking down the hall one day, in a previous church I led, and I had just admonished some guy. I told him the reason he was having problems in his Christian life was he wasn't coming to church enough. As I was walking along the Spirit of God spoke to me and said, 'John would you go here if you weren't paid?' I suddenly realized, 'No, I would not come here if I was not paid'. I ended up on my face, repenting before God and realizing that I had built an Ishmael, instead of an Isaac. While I was waiting for the Child of Promise, I begat a child of the flesh. If God has promised you, you wait for the real child, seek Him until you know. I hurt a lot of people without that other Child. I did a lot of damage, and it's still going on.

DEMOGRAPHIC RESEARCH: TARGET AREA

There are two related chapters on demographics. The first, this one, is actual research John draws on to analyze the current ministry target of the young Vineyard movement. The second provides you with the outline of what to research when doing a demographic analysis and how to obtain the information. We could call the first a 'case history' of demographic research and the second an outline of how to go about doing it.

A SUMMARY FROM GEORGE GALLUP JR. & DAVID POLING

In their book Gallup and Poling capsulate the results of their 1979 poll of religious belief in America. This section will give some of their major findings and seek some application to our own situation.

The first finding was that youth in the U.S. are vitally interested in religious faith. They are interested in real faith but criticize the institutional church for not living out its message. Most teenagers believe in God and have some religious practice (9 out of 10 polled pray). Yet only 1 in 4 indicated confidence in organized religion. Most youth have a very personal, individualistic approach to God, feeling that they can be good Christians without attending church. Like their parents they believe but do not belong. The young people have a burning desire to serve. They want to be involved in a cause demanding their all.

In the area of family, America seems to desire to return to traditional values. At the same time there is incredible trouble and breakdown in the American family. There is therefore a felt need for church programs that help take traditional family values and flesh them out. America is more traditional in many aspects than the media would lead us to believe. For example, only 9% of women in the U.S. want the 'career girl' lifestyle. There are many danger signs for the family. From 1970–80 the divorce rate doubled. The writers found American families spiritually illiterate. Yet a hopeful sign is that the parents seem to desire religious education for their children (75%).

The Catholic church is the major force in the religious arena. There are 48 million in the US! They grew from 25% of the population in 1970 to 28% in 1980. Within the Catholic church there is a growing openness to their separated brethren, the Protestants. There are some encouraging signs of life in the Catholic church such as prayer groups, bible studies, masses, lay renewal teams, and the charismatic movement.

The next major area of their poll was what they called the unchurched Christian. They found that the unchurched are overwhelmingly believers:

- They pray
- The believe in Jesus
- They think about life after death
- They believe the Easter story
- They want religious instruction.

But again, although they are strong believers, they don't belong or attend or support a local church. Gallup defined the unchurched as someone who didn't attend church in the last six months, except on holidays or special occasions. 41% of the adult population is unchurched in the U.S. (61 million people!). The adult population does seem to be seeking the true meaning of life, but only about half have any confidence that the church is the place to look. 88% believe you can be a good Christian without attending church.

There are forces which keep the unchurched from participating in church.

- Mobility
- Sports and recreational activity
- Social activities
- Work schedule
- Desire for more time for me and my family

Besides scheduling, the unchurched are also turned off by the following:

- Our beliefs are too narrow (37%)
- We are too focused on money (32%)
- They dislike traditional forms of worship (23%)

Despite all these barriers, 52% of the unchurched say they are open to becoming an active member of a church in the future.

Some of the reasons people join a church are:
- Friends invited them and they like the people
- Good preaching
- Good religious education for them or their family
- A personal religious experience
- Self-need

WHAT DOES THIS MEAN TO US IN THE VINEYARD?

The above section deals with some sociologically oriented material about what is going on in our country, what kind of people are out there, what kind of a response to anticipate. How do we relate this information to our context?

There is a vast market-place for us to tap. Those who believe but do not belong must be gathered and discipled. If they are not attracted to the traditional church the Vineyard package could reach them. They need reality in a contemporary package.

The *youth* in our country are open to a vital personal relationship with God. The harvest is truly ripe for young churches. The young people are ready to receive Christ all across the nation, in both Canada and the United States. They are hungry, very hungry. They are actualizes, they want to do, they don't want to just hear about it. But they will take hearing it if you will do it with them. They will only be attracted to a church that is living out the gospel. We must give them a place in the army of God, a cause to give their lives for!

The felt need in *the family* is an open door. We can reach into our community by providing help for their hurting families, but using seminars on marriage, parenting, and family life.

The Catholic church should be prayed for and encouraged and blessed. They are a major religious force in America. I think there are 65 million nominal Catholics in the United States, but only 13% of them go to church regularly. The bulk of them do not have a personal relationship with God. My preference would be that they would get one and stay in the Catholic Church, but the chances of that happening are somewhat remote. Short of that, I would rather win them and draw them into some vehicle that they can relate to, such as the Vineyard.

Those who believe but don't belong must be gathered and discipled. They are not attracted to the traditional church, but the Vineyard package could reach them. They need reality in a contemporary package. We have the power of the Holy Spirit to see lives changed and it is in a form they can relate to. The most effective way to reach them seems to be the invitation of a friend. We must train our people to reach out and invite.

Another key area is *children's ministry*. People will not stay at our churches if we do not provide 'religious' instruction. Although I am prejudiced, I believe we have a great opportunity and a perfect instrument to reach the unchurched in the U.S. The combination of power evangelism and contemporary forms of worship can win this generation. Religious instruction focuses on the disciplining of behavior from the outer to the inner. We can link that to the power of God from time to time as we bring our children along to lay hands on them. The Spirit of God visits them and hundreds of them are filled with the Holy Spirit. Whether they are 3 or 13, they experience God! On the one hand we give them instruction, satisfying their parents, and on the other hand we zap them with the power of God. We need both. Don't overlook the children as a resource. I have ministered to a large church in Texas. We brought the children forward at every service. The Spirit of God would just sweep in and touch them so beautifully, fill them and they would prophecy and speak in tongues. It was lovely 6, 7, 8, 9, 10 and 12 year-old kids prophesying. 'Suffer the little children to come unto Me.'

DEMOGRAPHICS

Why engage in demographic studies?
- To identify people groups
- To determine receptivity
- To know the people you are trying to reach.

The more you know about them, the easier it is to reach them. It is just like going fishing.

WHAT INFORMATION DO YOU NEED?

What information is helpful to know about the community God has called you to?

People on the move are easy to win for Christ. They are also the hardest to keep in your church. The average person in our church has moved every year for the past five years. We struggle to keep up with their addresses. We are ministering to a transit population. As a result, we have a big front door and a big back door. They are all on their way through. No one is going to stay. So, I give little energy to make them stay. I try to group them as they stay.

Growth trends

What percentage of the population changes every year? What is the recent history of patterns of change in the population? Some areas have 80% turn over every year. This is where it is easy to evangelize, but hard to build a church. There is not enough of a stable population.

Characteristics of the community

Investigate,
- Employment

- Commuting patterns
- Traffic patterns.

Then, when you choose your venue, it should conform to their patterns. A person can travel 35 miles to work and go back there at night to church, but he will not go somewhere else, which is actually nearer, but not perceived to be nearer. You need to understand how they think.

Investigate area divisions in the community,

- Age
- Income
- Race

Population characteristics

What type of people are they? How do they think? What is the actual demographic break down, but also, does their recent history (where they just moved from) determine their mentality? Determine percentages that are,

- Urban
- Suburban, or
- Rural?

Investigate,

- Population growth rate (last ten years). Some city areas are declining. But they still have a few million people.
- Population projection (next ten years).

Characteristics of target group

Family characteristics

- Age of head of household.

You can easily meet and minister to people roughly your age (up to ten years younger or older). Determine how many spouses work. Some churches try to start women's bible studies where 70% of the people work every day. In upper class areas you can start such bible studies, but not in communities where both spouses work. You must fish with hooks that are related to the fish. Some churches just borrow models that worked elsewhere, with no demographic understanding.

- Children: number, ages
- Marriage patterns
- Profession
- Personnel interests, attitudes
- Political bias
- Hobbies, leisure activities
- Personal concerns, needs and felt needs: obtained through a survey

Socio-economic level

I was with a church in the Bronx. They wanted to start home bible studies. But the Bronx looks like Berlin after the 2nd World War. This church spent two years trying to start bible studies, because the pastor had gone to a conference where they told him this was the way to run a successful church. However, he had never bothered to ask about the socio-economic level of communities where home groups work well.

I went to a church once where they had been told the way to successful ministry was to run a bus ministry. They went out and bought 6 buses and almost went broke. They had not thought at all about demographics.

Church related information

Determine the church/population ratio. We have about 340,000 churches in the USA. In California we have 23 million people, and 23,00 churches, 1 for every 100,000 people. In the rural areas it is 1 to 300. The urban areas don't have churches. That would be good news if you were fishing. Here they are, all between this highway and that highway.

Determine,

- Protestant church to population ratio
- Unchurched population
- Number of churches in area
- Size of churches
- Growth rate
- Denominational spread
- Ethnic make-up

DEMOGRAPHICS

How do I find demographic information?

- County halls, library
- Chamber of Commerce
- City Hall, city information booths
- School districts
- Development companies (especially in planned communities)
- Commercial and marketing companies
    - Utility companies
    - Newspapers, magazines: sales and research department
    - Local radio stations
    - Real Estate boards
- Census Bureau
- Personal study: community studies
- Church information
    - Newspapers
    - Chamber of Commerce
    - Phone book
    - Council of churches

What is the relevance of this information? The Lord often says, 'go to that city' but does not tell you where in that city. That is where this is helpful. It is not essential, but it is helpful.

THE INGREDIENTS OF A NEW CHURCH

LEADERSHIP STYLE AND TEMPERAMENT

The way a person leads is called style

The first point to consider is 'How could I lead'. What are the different ways that a person could lead? As we go through these points, you will discern some of your own strengths and weaknesses. Hopefully it will help you find out, not only who you are and what you need to do, but how to change as your groups grow. You probably have a model in mind, but this will help you to understand the need for diversity or change.

Leadership styles should be understood in the context of a contrasting grid, as follows.

Comfortable	Uncomfortable
Democratic	Autocratic
Agreeable	Motivational
Directionless	Directional

Autocratic

Normally people have an entirely negative view of an autocratic leader. However, there might be a time when you need to operate as an autocratic leader.

An autocratic person is seen as a dictator, authoritative, operating from a chain of command and is often a strong decision maker. As you know, if a person operates only in an autocratic style it can be dangerous and detrimental to people. It could be as dangerous and detrimental to you as the person who is leading. An autocrat will tend to attract a certain type of individual, who is then reproduced in the church. Some would say you are casting your bread on the water. It will come back to you. I like to be nice to people. The main reason is I like people to be nice to me. It seems to be a people principle that what you give out is what you will get back.

Democratic

The autocratic is contrasted with the democratic. The democratic person is normally viewed as benevolent. He helps other people make decisions. Often democratic leaders are directed by those they are trying to serve.

Motivational

The motivational leader stands in contrast to the agreeable. A motivational leader is often viewed as manipulative. I have heard people say, 'he isn't trying to motivate me, he's trying to manipulate me.' Such leaders are charismatic, winsome, people with good persuasion skills. Usually they are attractive, people who have the ability to draw people to themselves. They are often talkers. They talk and talk and talk, trying to get people to do things.

Note, these are the ways such leaders are viewed. They may not actually be like that.

Agreeable

An agreeable person is viewed as quiet, mild, meditative, someone who thinks through things before making a decision. They usually make decisions with you in mind. They are supportive and are good listeners.

Directional

The directional leader is viewed as strong and opinionated. He takes firm action and tells people what to do. He is also a person that easily confronts. Such a person makes up his mind real quick and then tells you what you need to do, or what the group should do. Sometimes it is of God, while at other times it is not.

Directionless

Directionless leaders are viewed as unconcerned, lacking focus, dull, unsure and lacking in clear goals, or with a weakness in setting goals.

Application

I have seen people actually try to minister in all six categories, but usually specializing in one. They often insist that what they are is what God wants a pastor to be like. Some people think that the pastor ought to rule. Other people think that the pastor ought to ask people where they want to go and then lead them accordingly. Some people see the pastor as someone that is supportive and a good listener. Other people see a pastor as a leader that is pointing the way, saying this is what you should do. People tend to take on the leadership style of those who have led them. If that was done to them, they will assume, 'this is the way God does it.' Or they were told it was that way, or they assumed the role unconsciously.

The point here it to become conscious of which style you actually manifest. Then try to see the strengths of the alternative to your own style. If you are an autocratic person, are you going to learn how to help others to be involved in the decision-making process? If you are a directionless person there are going to be times when people will need somebody to stand up and say, 'this is the way we are going'. A leader who is uncertain will make people insecure.

Have you ever played that game on roller skates or ice skates, where you get in a line and follow the person in front? All of a sudden, the front person turns, and the G force hits the last person, making it slam him into the snow-bank. We played it when we were kids. There are always people at the end. As a leader you can turn really quickly, like on a dime. It doesn't affect you. You don't have any pressures exerted on you. Then you realize you are losing people. Some people have been lost because of the whiplash effect.

People that are motivational, autocratic and directional are viewed as aggressive types. They also are viewed as assertive. The people on the other side are viewed as passive. That is the style of leadership they normally portray. Another word is congenial.

These styles then relate to what is appropriate for different kinds of churches and different stages of church growth. If you are an assertive, aggressive person, the church better grow fairly quickly. Such leaders are difficult to take in the context of a small group. Normally the type of temperament that works best in the small group is a congenial, passive type leader. Such leaders then must face the consequences of their own success. Pretty soon they have 30, 40, 50 people. I get phone calls like this. They say, 'Hey we have 20–25 people up here in … we'd like somebody to come up that is more assertive, more aggressive. We need a new type of leader now.' So, there is a place for everybody.

There are times when you need to learn how to be the other style, if you can, because if you are always aggressive, always assertive, you also will violate people. There need to be times when you are congenial, when you are nice too.

We have a concept of a leader in America. It contrasts with what Jesus Christ said about being a servant. People often assume that the congenial and passive are servant types, while the other two are not. I do not find that to be true. I do not think that is what Jesus is saying. You can be an assertive person who serves people. You can be aggressive and serve them, or congenial, or passive.

You need to learn how to change as a group grows. You need to be more congenial with those who are leading with you. You've got to give people a place in the sun. If you hog the whole thing you will find that you will be losing leadership types all the time. They won't stay with you and it isn't their fault. We may see them as rebellious because they are not doing what we want them to do. Diversity is important.

2 Timothy 2:2 is a text that describes the process of multiplication, how to reproduce yourself in the life of someone else.

> And the things you have heard me say in the presence of many witnesses entrust to reliable men who will also be qualified to teach others.

This text is used to support various discipleship programs. The theme is, make people like you. The strength and qualities you have, do that to someone else and have them go out and do it to other people.

There is another concept called equipping. What an equipper does is to look at a person's life and sense the anointing upon that person, the calling of God, the skills and temperament of a person. The equipper helps to develop and release that person. This is the Ephesians 4 model.

> It was he who gave some to be apostles, some to be prophets, some to be evangelists, and some to be pastors and teachers, to prepare God's people for works of service, so that the body of Christ may be built up until we all reach unity in the faith and in the knowledge of the Son of God and become mature, attaining to the whole measure of the fullness of Christ (Ephesians 4:11–13).

Often what we do is we disciple people and then ask Jesus to equip them afterwards. I do not think people have to be like us. They should be nurtured to become like Jesus. Of course, there is truth in the 2 Timothy principle. If we follow Jesus, then we have a certain quality of Christian life. I am not talking about sinlessness. I am talking about being a model of ministry. We may function so well in this model of ministry that others ought to function like we do. However, as I read the Scriptures, Jesus Christ is to be the example. We are to function like He did. If we try and sense what God has done in people's lives, then we can help them become what God has called them to be.

Many leaders fall into the habit of calling people into ministry. The church is filled with those today. People called us and told us to go into a certain ministry. Then they feel like failures because they couldn't do it, but it wasn't God that called them. Men called them, and because they love people, because they desired to teach, they were told they ought to be a pastor.

In summary

First of all diversity is needed. Secondly try to figure out what type of person you normally are and these characteristics will help you. Those of you who are single are going to have a more difficult time than those who are married. For men in leadership, wives are very good at helping us understand who we really are. When I meet with pastors, I always tell them 'bring your wife because I want to know the truth.' I don't know about you guys, but if my wife's not around I tell some good stories. If she is there, I catch myself in the middle of a story and she's standing directly by my side. I go, 'oh, that's not really true, is it.' I hate being honest all the time. It's not fun. The way I dream seems more real and more important than who I really am.

Three types of pastors

I believe the epitaph on the gravestone of a Christian ought to be 'Learner' not 'Learned.'

The catalyst

A catalyst is basically a starter, a person who starts things. Some will say, 'oh, it takes a charismatic person to be a catalyst'. Not always. Some who are timid, or the congenial types, are the leaders initially. They are able to draw people with leadership skills around them, and together they become a powerful charismatic unit. The catalyst is the person who doesn't just start things, but also causes things to gel, to come together. A catalyst is the type of person that thinks they can organize, but they don't have time. Often this kind of person will be viewed as undisciplined. Catalysts feel that they are starting so many things—that's all they like to do by the way—they have 10 things going, all they need do is get them organized sufficiently to make them operate. People will tell them, 'stop doing so many things'. Have you ever tried to stop gravity? It just flows. So it is with the catalyst.

The organizer

An organizer is a person who does just that. If an organizer was to come into this room he would say, 'hold it, this room is messy. This should go here, this there.' An organizer has the ability to see things that are out of sorts, or out of control. Organizers think they can start things, but they are so busy organizing they never get to do it, or hardly ever get to do it. They love to organize something that has been started, something that is there already. Consequently, they are seen as very disciplined.

As well as understanding these types of leaders, we need to understand the dynamics that occur between them, as they inter-relate.

Let me give you an analogy, let's say doing paving. A catalyst is like the person who lays the asphalt down. Asphalt is very hot. They have special boots with a substance in them trying to make their feet as cool as possible. This guy is wearing these boots and he has this hand roller. Before he had a power-tool he used to roll these things by hand. He would get blisters on his feet and get tired. You cannot work for very long in that condition. All of a sudden the person is thinking, 'this is crazy, my feet are hot, they ache because of all this heat. What if we could put wheels on this thing? Then I could stand on it and push it along.' In his mind he can see this machine. It has wheels and a motor on it. So, he starts talking to people about it. 'Hey, this could be a great thing'. Usually he thinks up a series of prototypes. He never makes one, he just thinks of a lot of different ways you could do it. Then he talks to an organizer, perhaps an architect or architectural engineer. He draws it. He puts it together. But the problem is, he doesn't like to run it.

The maintainer

The maintainer thinks he can start and organize, but normally the best thing they can do, following our illustration, is hold the wheel. A maintainer is a person who likes to run what somebody else has organized.

THE INGREDIENTS OF A NEW CHURCH

This guy would like to drive a steam roller, would like to oil one, keep it going, but he really doesn't have what it takes to come up with the idea, nor is he capable of making his own one. He doesn't have what it takes to draw it or make the dream become a reality.

As you grew up in the church, what type of leader predominated? The maintainer! For years seminaries have been turning out maintainers. It's not that they are wrong. It's just that they met the ecclesiastical need. The last time there was revival here in America was in 1902 to 1906. Many things were started and organized. Since then the church has moved into maintenance mode. However, I think most of us are disillusioned with the present organization. We do not want to be maintainers. Young people want to start things. Have you ever seen the Fidelity Savings commercial? The older guy is talking to his buddy on the golf course. My son called me the other day and told me about his recent investment. He said 'my money is in Fidelity, I know it's safe and I don't want to risk anymore.' He is developing an over 40 mentality, a retirement mentality, which is different from a person between 20 and 30. They are thinking of starting things and building things. An older person is thinking of winding things down, maintaining what they've got.

That is what is happening in the church. About ten years ago, when I noticed this, I started putting the emphasis on organizers, functional people, people with administrative skills. Most pastors are not good business people. They make poor decisions and those decisions, especially financial ones, kill the church. The problem is, there haven't been a lot of catalysts. But things are changing. In the last ten years a lot of new churches have started.

Whether you like this or not, organizers have a tough time with catalytic people. Maintainers can't stand them! Some of you have been in denominational churches where there have been maintainers in leadership. You've had all these ideas, and they keep taking it away, trying to take away your toys. They say, quoting years of experience, 'it doesn't work'—whatever your idea is. The older you get, even though you may be a catalytic person, the more you will become a dreamer. Old men have dreams. They are not visions any more, they are dreams. Those who go out to start a church will tend to be catalytic people. Most of the churches in town will have organizers and maintainers. It's not that they don't like you or don't like somebody coming to town. That is not really what they are upset about. It's what you represent. They cannot understand why you want to start something when they already have something going.

Churches go through stages. Normally those who start churches are catalysts. The key is for the catalyst to leave behind organizers and maintainers. What has hardly ever worked is when an organizer starts a church. Some organizers can start churches, but fewer church plants are led by organizers than by catalysts. The idea is to free a catalyst, but normally the catalyst will drive you nuts. After a period of time you will not appreciate what they have done, because they could start something, but they couldn't put it together. If you or someone else starts to organize it, it starts looking good. When the church starts, the catalyst looks like a hero. Why? Because they are normally the ones who can gather people. But after a while, if you are only a catalyst, you will ruin people. A church starts. Everybody is happy, with 40–50 people in the place. Then you move out of the house and get into a larger building. Now you have 100 people. Previously nobody was really concerned about not having the children attended to adequately. Some of them brought children and some of them were taken care of elsewhere. Now people want something to be organized for the children. Others want something for the youth. People begin to ask, 'What is going on here?' What is going to happen? What is our focus? What is our vision?' The catalytic person tends to operate out of intuition. You ask them for reasons why they are doing what they do and they cannot give you a reason. That doesn't mean it is not of God. They do not know how to answer your questions but what they do is right.

In summary then, once a church has started, the time comes when organizers are required. The trick is to have the catalyst release the organizer. Another kind of person can be described as the feeder. They will feed the church. They will initiate functional structures. This type of person wants to know exactly why things are going to happen, what will happen, and where the parameters are. But the catalyst finds them frustrating. They say, 'don't ask so many questions. You're questioning the Holy Spirit.' I just visited a church in Arizona where these dynamics were in play. The pastor is a catalyst. He has an organizer that is a good friend. But he said his friend was driving him crazy. The church was fairly well organized already. Now this fellow wants to arrange everything differently. He keeps adding to it. The reason is, the leader is a catalyst, who now has an organizer, but they do not have a maintainer. The organizer keeps looking for new things to organize, but there is no one to maintain what has been organized.

Generally, maintainers cannot release catalysts. Often God speaks but we cannot hear because of who we are. God wants everybody to be important, not just one person. There are those who will hear God when certain things need to happen, while others will be incapable of hearing God because of who they are. Often when a group needs to be organized the catalyst cannot hear it. Alternatively, when a catalyst needs to be sent out, a maintainer cannot hear it.

NATURAL PROCESS AND PERCEPTION

THREE STAGES THAT A GROUP GOES THROUGH

Personal and spiritual growth

This also may be characterized as the development of character, or the fruits of the Holy Spirit. Most people, before they find Christ, want to change, but they do not know how to do it or how let others do it with them. In meeting their personal and spiritual needs you lead them to Christ. They become born again Christians. Once they are Christians they want to change even more. They have a desire to grow in Christ, a desire to change. I often ask people, 'Why did you come to this church? Why aren't you in another church?' They say, 'Well, I don't know why I'm not in some of the other churches, I know I did try some, but when I came here I sensed that I could change here. This group would let me change. They had information, they had things that would help me grow personally and spiritually, and that's what I wanted.'

Ministry—Anointing, Gifts of the Spirit

After people have some of their personal spiritual needs met, they start thinking about ministering to others. So, ministry becomes prominent in their lives. They start developing an interest in language like 'anointing,' or 'gifts of the Holy Spirit.' Now they want to be used of God to help others change, because they like what's happened to them. It's natural. This is when the group wants to visit seminars on how to discover your spiritual gifts, or they want to work through material like that in the group.

Vision & Mission

Once people have been equipped in some measure they become interested in mission. Mission could be that Jesus sends us to evangelize our friends, or it may be an interest in the ministry of healing. The people of the group begin to catch the overall mission of the church they are in: evangelism, church planting, or perhaps ministry to the poor. They want to begin to make a difference in the world.

Discerning the Stages

Problems develop when we can no longer discern which stage we should be focused on, or when we think that we can never go backwards to a previous stage.

When you are 'on a mission' you tend to become absorbed by it to the extent that you begin to deny your own personal and spiritual needs. For instance, while in worship you are thinking about the sermon you are going to give. When you study the Scriptures you are not thinking about how it applies to your own life, but how you can help other peoples' lives. This can be a trap. Ministry normally isn't a trap, but when people get a sense of vision or a mission that God has called them to, especially pastors, they can become fixated on their mission. You get caught up in doing it and doing it and doing it to others. Then, when your wife or children or someone else in the group says, 'I hurt', you get angry with them. They are leaving the front lines of the battle, where you are so busy!

I remember one ministry trip when ten of us were going to go. Then when the time came, only three of us were there. The other seven didn't make it because they were into their 'hurts.' They were going through relational stress, or financial stress. The 'enemy' used distraction to sap them of their strength. I don't know how many pastors' wives have said to me that the reason they are not successful is because they just did not have the energy to commit to the vision any longer. They wanted to have relationship, they wanted to get healed up some more. So they felt like the men were failures thought their wives. In truth, there was absolutely nothing wrong with them. They just had a valid felt need.

Some of you have started small churches, and some of you have yet to start churches. Remember this. As people start ministering, they tend to forget what is important, including how they got there. The mission becomes all-important. You talk about denying your needs, or your feelings, or dying to self, for the sake of the mission.

The point is this: it is OK to go back to stage one, even if you have reached stage three. It's OK to go back and get healed up and slow down the mission. If you allow people to go back and get healed, then they will get strengthened and refreshed to serve once more. They will become committed to you and the vision once more. Sometimes you lose your own vision. Then you realize what is wrong, you get healed up and you start ministering again. You get back into focus and rediscover your calling.

For some reason many pastors feel it is wrong to go back and get healing, as though it will show weakness. They must always to appear to be strong, to be the person carrying the flag. Some will ask what 'going back' means. Do you mean the person has to leave the mission and go back to another church or someplace where they can be cured? Yes, it can sometimes require that. We have something like sixty to seventy pastors in our church. They were so focused on mission they got beat up, or abused by Christians. Sometimes the enemy was using the church to break them down. They had no desire to read their Scriptures anymore. They didn't want to come to worship. They didn't want to do anything that had a spiritual context to it. Seminaries are often to blame. They were told; don't let people know you are hurt. They will use it against you.

Many pastors in churches have been caught up in adultery, financial excess, or going back into homosexuality or some other lust. One of the biggest things that pastors of pastors can do (APC's[2]) is to provide relationship. Forget your regional agenda if necessary. You need relationship! You need a healing environment where it is OK to tell people where you are at and let people minister to you. It is best if you can find people in your church to share with. I am not talking about self-disclosing to a large group. I am talking about relational small groups where people can really help you.

I have always valued being able to come to a small group meeting. Here I am, a pastor of a church, with an expectation on me to always be focused on the mission. Recently Cindy Rethmeier was doing the worship at the Denunzio's house. We have another group at our house now, but this was our previous group. I could go to that group at any time and say 'hey you guys I'm not certain that God is still alive. I haven't heard from him all week. I have been so busy ministering and taking care of people. I haven't read my Bible, any of you guys know about that? I really haven't prayed except to tell God about some of the needs these people have, but not really to develop intimacy with Him. So, if any of you have a sense of what God wants to do, do it. I'm going to go over to the corner and get into a fetal position and suck my thumb'. Literally, sometimes I would just lie on the floor, and they would minister to me. On this occasion it was not long

---

[2] Area Pastoral Coordinator, one of the Vineyard leadership roles for pastoring pastors.

before Cindy and her husband Steve and the Denunzio's and others started sensing that they were involved in this thing too. They would identify with me and pray about things in my life. It is not that I am unstable. I probably did something like that three times in two years, but the first time I did, it shocked them to death.

As pastors of churches we need the same thing. We need to have a place where we can go and say, 'hey, you guys, you know I'm just confused right now, I just don't know what to do, I need to be protected'. That is too intimate for some of you. However, if your small group never gets to be real you will be trapped in it. It will either stop growing, or it will start revolving. People will spin out. Pastors that get trapped in unreality will find that their churches will not continue to grow.

In summary, groups go through stages. You will never have everybody in phase 3. In fact, it is dangerous as a leader to try and get everybody in phase 3. Some of the people in your church will be in phase 1, some in phase 2, some in phase 3. If you're a growing church the percentages will be more people in phase 1 than in 2 or 3.

Type of Church	Phase 1	Phase 2	Phase 3
Young, growing church	70%	20%	10%
More mature church	50%	40%	10%
Imaginary church	20%	40%	40%

We tend to always be trying to get people to phase 3. Don't do that. Just minister to their needs! As churches start growing we forget we are in the business of ministering to people. We keep thinking about 'building the church', and we stop ministering to the people. You wonder why people don't come anymore, or why we don't reach any new ones. It is because we are so involved in our focus on ministry and mission, instead of just helping people.

GROUP PERCEPTIONS

The group is perceived from three different positions. At any given time, the following three perceptions apply to a group:

- Group projection—those inside the group
- Group impression—those outside the group

- Group image—the individual inside the group

Group projection—those inside the group

First, there is the projection of the group, what you think you are doing to a community. Most churches think that what they are trying to do to the community is important. But they do not check out the impressions they have created.

Group impression—those outside the group

We tend not ask people outside the church 'how do we come across to you?' What if their perception is of a group that is critical and judgmental, when you think you are coming across loving? I had a problem and I came to you and you told me what a sinner I was and that God was going to get me. I could see in your eyes you didn't like me.' Conversely sometimes you think you came across fairly harshly, and people say 'no, I needed that. I didn't sense any hatred or dislike, it came across right'. We tend to be hung up in our projection and unaware of the outside impression of our group. Further, we tend to think that we come across as a whole, as a group or church, rather than a diverse set of individuals. Then we wonder why we can't reach the community.

Group Image—the individual inside the group

Often the leader is caught up in self-perception while the people inside the group do not believe in the image you think the group is projecting. They do not believe that you are really loving, or caring, or all these things you are trying to project to the community. You are not even doing it in the church, much less outside. Image is something that you are always doing. You are always saying 'Here is who we are, here is what we are about'. There are two ways to check it out. Ask the people outside the church (group impression), ask the people inside the church (group image). If you can do it in a way that people will not be found out, they will probably be more honest. They will tell you how you are coming across.

TYPES OF PEOPLE TO BE REACHED

Initially some people are easier to reach earlier on, while others come later. When you start a church, the people that are most open are those you might consider unstable and helpless.

NATURAL PROCESS AND PERCEPTION

'Unstable' or 'helpless'

They do not look like something you could build a church on, and in fact, you can't. It is not that those people are not valuable. All I am saying is you can't build a church on them. If people are unstable and feeling helpless, what will happen when your group grows to 25-30 people? You will counsel day in and day out, week in, week out, month in, month out, year in, year out, for years. You will be caught up in counseling. It is a trap pastors get caught into. We think we are called to counsel and we are not. Many churches stop growing because pastors get caught up in counseling. There are people in your church that are difficult to help. You will be caught up in their need and have no time left to minister to other types of people.

Stable but somewhat helpful

This is where you can find some leaders that can help you minister to the first type. If you try and be the answer man, the answer woman, the savior to the people, you will attract a certain type of person that will leaven the whole. Most people do not want to come to a church where most of the people are miserable. When you start, you will attract a type of person that will come to anything that's going. They are so hurting that their need causes them to come in. You must realize that you can't help all their needs initially, you've got to build a church to help meet all those needs. If you let those needs overwhelm you, you won't build a church that can really minister to them later.

I have cried many times. I have realized the constant need of the people and the reality that we cannot help them all. We just have to say, 'I can't help you.' They will say 'but surely there is power in the blood of Jesus Christ'. We have to say to some, 'I agree, but I don't know how to do it in your case. I don't know how to release it, I don't have what it takes to help you'. We know we should, we are not there yet. You will go through that frustration over and over and over again.

Very stable and helpful

This type normally does not come first. They usually come into a community that is somewhat organized and helping each other. They will come from other churches where the burden was beyond them and they don't want to get in a cage again. They have had their time ministering. It hurts so much they don't want to get into it again. If we create a system where the people are free to minister or not to minister, then they will eventually venture out again. Some of you had those people in your churches but you could not figure out why they did not want to get involved with you. The reason is, they got burnt where they came from. If you provide a flexible, free system for them to minister or not, then they will go with you.

Such a flexible, growing system should work something like this.

Skilled Leadership Model

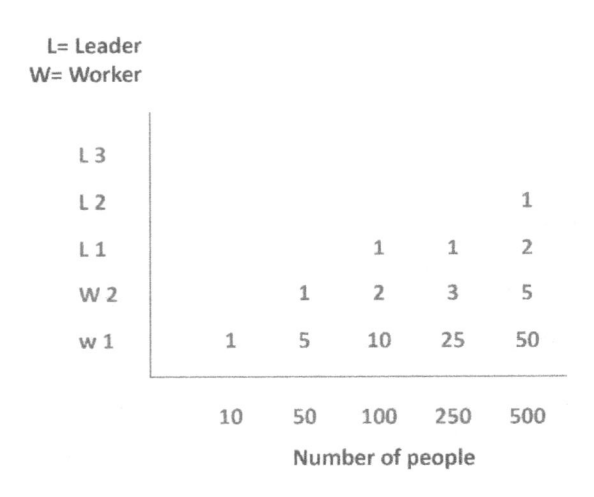

L= Leader
W= Worker

L 3					
L 2					1
L 1			1	1	2
W 2		1	2	3	5
w 1	1	5	10	25	50
	10	50	100	250	500

Number of people

On average, within the context of small groups, one giving, caring type of person can look after a maximum of 10 other people. A good Christian couple can often do that. Such people do not need much training. They require fundamental relational skills that come naturally to most. This means we have a proportion to 1:10 at the level of basic caring, or what we have called a W1.

As you multiply groups, and as more people come, you need to maintain that proportion, so a church of 50 needs five W1 workerss, 100 needs 10, 250 needs 25, and 500 needs 50.

If we view this from the end of the process, what happens when you have 50 workers? Who is going to care for them? This means we must build into the system a way of caring for the workers. Here the proportion needs to be different, because a worker has different needs to the people on the ground. Here we need a proportion of about 1 to 5. For every five W1 workers we need one person to work with them. This kind of person needs more skills. The ideal is to have people who have been successful W1 workers, and who can now mentor others doing what they have done. So, we call these W2 level workers. They look after a group of leaders that each look after a small group. For a church of 100 you need 2 W2 workers. At this point the founding pastor will probably be that W2 worker but will be drawing someone alongside to assist. You might break the 10 W1 workers into two groups of 5, and have each one care for a group of 5. For a church of 250 your need at least three W2 workers. At this point the founding pastor may have added to the staff, so that an associate is one of the W2 workers.

Now you are beginning to have a group of W2 workers. Who is going to care for them? The ability to care for this level of worker requires more skills. At this level you really need leadership skills. You need to be able to give training to your workers. You need discernment to determine who can and cannot be raised up as W1 and W2 workers. So, we call this a L1 leader. The skills have moved beyond caring, to leadership training and development. When the church is small the founding pastor is the first L1 level leader, and can sustain that role for a while, as the church grows, merely adding to the W2 level workers. However, the point will come when there needs to be a number of L1 leaders. At this point the founding pastor becomes team leader of a staff made up of professionally paid, part time and volunteer leaders. To lead such a staff team requires yet more skill. At this point we have a L2 leader.

And so the process should continue. The point is, as the founding pastor, or church planter, you have to keep reinventing yourself, from being the first W1 who cares for 10 people, to a W2 who cares for a group of small group leaders, to a L1 who begins to train and equip workers, to a staff team leader. You must keep multiplying yourself and what you have learned to do in ministry to people, into others, who catch what you do and then do it to others. You will find that whatever you did to people, to love and care for them and help them in their journey, they will do again to others. Whatever you did to support workers, they will do to others when they have the same responsibility. The style they have will be different to yours, so you will have to learn to 'give it away' again and again. You may struggle to give it away, fearing that the people will not be loved and cared for as you would do it yourself, but unless you give away the ministry you will be overwhelmed, and the church will not grow.

To achieve this you have to keep changing yourself. The role of a person who cares for 10 people is quite different from a leader of leaders. You have to evolve in order for the church to grow. You must learn to raise up leaders and release ministry to them, otherwise your church will hit a ceiling and never grow any larger. In this process your own style will have to change. Someone who loves 10 people is very relational and congenial. But a leader of 1000 cannot always be congenial.

NATURAL EMERGING LEADERS

Where do you find leaders then?

Those you have ministered to

You will be drawn naturally to those you have ministered to and they in turn will be drawn to you. These will be people you like, and who like you.

Those with a calling

Then out of that group, you begin to inquire into what God has called people to? What passions has he placed within them? What gifts has he bestowed on them? We have always taught that we need to pray over people and see what God was doing in their life. What was He calling them to? What anointing has he placed on them? In the beginning it may be an intuition you have about someone, a perception. Then you try to test it and see if it is a reality. Sometimes the friends you first drew around you and ministered to will become associate staff in the church and then become pastoral staff with you. Or they may go out and start their own church, because God has used you to raise them up from among the leaders.

Those with formal training

Once you are up into L1 or L2 leadership, formal training has to come in.
We like to emphasize what we call the Ephesians 4 model.

> But to each one of us grace has been given as Christ apportioned it … When he ascended on high, he led captives in his train and gave gifts to men … It was he who gave some to be apostles, some to be prophets, some to be evangelists, and some to be pastors and teachers, to prepare God's people for works of service, so that the body of Christ may be built up until we all reach unity in the faith

and in the knowledge of the Son of God and become mature, attaining to the whole measure of the fullness of Christ (Ephesians 4:7-13).

To prepare people for works of service we need a blend of formal training and mentoring, where we show people how to do it, because we have done it before them. When you mentor people you can tell them what it feels like. They can understand, they can relate with you. If I haven't pastured you, then I cannot know what some of you are feeling like as you pastor others.

There is one final warning I need to give you about those who come in with formal training already. As your church grows through the process of W1 and W2 workers, to the need for L1 and L2 leaders, people will come into your church from outside to help you minister, to accomplish your vision. Sometimes we think this is a big deal. Most of the time it is trouble. This is the kind of problem that can lead to churches splitting. Experienced leaders coming into your church from outside will be people you have not ministered to yourself. They have not been part of the W1 stage.

I have heard horror stories recently of pastors that say that as they started to build their church, they were up to about 100 or 150, and this person came in because of the crowds. They started ministering right by their side and then took half their church within six months. So, watch out when people come in and want to go straight to the L1 or L2 level. The point is, you cannot lead people you have not ministered to. That is the bottom line. You cannot lead people you cannot minister to or have not ministered to. Don't let them assume a place of leadership in the church. If you give it to them and then try and take it away once they have established relationship with the people, you will have a fight on your hands.

BUILDING A CHURCH

The next section of the original material deals with 'Building a Church' and covers the now classic language of values, priorities, practices, programs and personnel. This section will not be incorporated. First, it was given a more thorough treatment by Wimber himself in a series called the 'Five Year Plan.' Second, this material, originally written up for John by Alexander Venter, is now incorporated in his publication, *Doing Church*.

THE DISCIPLESHIP PHASE

The process of discipleship is absolutely fundamental to church planting. It is the one ingredient you cannot do without. It is essential to the process of gathering, growing, training and sending people.

THE PATTERN OF JESUS' MINISTRY

Jesus was the first apostle, sent from the Father (Hebrews 3:1). Ultimately this is where our sense of mission begins. We are sent by him, just as he was sent by the Father (John 20:21).

Many people followed him and became disciples (John 8:31). But not all people who start, finish. Not all people that begin keep on keeping on. Ultimately, we have to measure those who stick. Good wishes don't help get the job done.

One time I preached in a church saying 'commitment is spelt m-o-n-e-y.' Where their money is, their hearts are. I said: 'I don't have your hearts. I can tell, by the way you give.' It was difficult, but it had to be confronted. I have got to teach the people to give. If they don't know how to give, they don't know how to live.

THE TWELVE APOSTLES

During Jesus ministry on earth, he developed some followers. Out of all the disciples, Jesus designated only twelve as apostles (Luke 6:13).

The functional use of 'apostle'

The three synoptic writers used the term 'functionally' to describe the Twelve after sending them out into trans-local kingdom ministry (Matthew 10:2; Mark 6:30; Luke 9:10).

There are two dynamics of ministry: Local and trans-local. Jesus ultimately sent them out to do trans-local ministry, but first he discipled them. Mark, the earliest writer, explains why Jesus chose them—mainly that they would be with him.

> He appointed twelve--designating them apostles--that they might be with him and that he might send them out to preach and to have authority to drive out demons (Mark 3:14–15).

Are you really with him? Lately God has been teaching me to pray. I feel really 'with him' right now, so in love with Jesus. There are times when you are closer than at other times. It is glorious. We need these times of refreshing and intimacy. I was losing my stretch, getting tired. When I was in Houston the Lord woke me up and told me to get close to him. It is great just to be in love with Jesus again. The first thing a disciple is, is a lover of God, talking to him, feeling his feeling, his burdens. I was praying about you people. He said, 'tell them to be close to me.' We think, 'well I want to go out and do things for you, this big plan I have.' He says, well, 'why don't we just be friends first. Sit down here and worship at my feet.' Before you do anything, you have to love him. All this effort, we are going to lay down one day. It will all burn.

Jesus built them up and trained them by modeling. Have you ever noticed how they looked like the three stooges? They were always confused about what he really was teaching, not understanding his motives, getting it all wrong. Are you not glad your weaknesses have not been paraded for posterity, like theirs were?

He demonstrated what he wanted them to be. In the way he taught, in the way he would go off and pray all night to the Father. The pattern of Jesus life is to be the pattern of your life. His word to us is, 'Do what I did.'

Scholars are agreed that the functional sense of apostles was being used here, to show the nature of their ministry. People do what you do, not what you tell them to do!

I was talking to a pastor in Fort Worth. He said, 'I want the power of God. I want to be a mouse in your pocket.' I told him, 'I will be in Dallas next week, and you can spend 86 hours with me. We are going to cast out demons, heal the sick, preach the kingdom, lead people to Christ, then after lunch we will …' He blinked. He said, 'you really do those things?' I said, 'yes right here in Dallas!' That is what I do. People need Jesus.

I have my failures. I was weeping over a child who is vegetating. We prayed and prayed and nothing happened. But this week there were people who were blind and now see, deaf and now can hear, legs that grew, teeth that grew, pastors who were broken and God restored them.

My advise to you is, get yourself a job, then give your evenings to Jesus. Or give your days to Jesus and get a night job. Find some place you have to actually do it. If you want people to pray, you must pray. If you want people to lead people to Christ, you must do it. Jesus wanted people to do what he was doing. This is what he told them when he commissioned them. Whatever you want your people to be, you be it.

Trans-local ministry

There are a lot of people out there who are 'saved' but not really saved. They don't know the difference between the cross, the blood and the tri-lateral commission! They have undergone a little change, but not that significant. Jesus has called us to a radical commitment to him. It may mean giving up some of our toys, for the rest of our lives. But most would rather have the praise of men than the praise of him. We must be clear what we are calling people to. So walk with the people! Do it with them. It is just like learning how to ride a bike. Let's do it again and again, until they learn it.

The process of discipleship with Jesus went, in summary, like this:

- Jesus built up a leadership team of around him (the twelve).
- Then he trained them until he had a viable base, a ministry team.
- Then used them to reach the multitudes.

He sent them right back into their own turf, into Galilee. Go north, go do it, then we will get together again and talk about it. Before he sent them, they had had a taste of what it was like.

- First, he did it in front of them.
- Then he got them to do it.
- Then he sent them to do it on their own.
- He then sent them forth into trans-local kingdom ministry.

This was their mission activity. He sent them out as teams. He broke them up, first 12, then 70 (72). Once he had laid hands on them, they came under anointing, with great signs and wonders following. They then came back to the base, after this excursion, to report back. Then he sent them out on more teams.

There will always be doubt, fear and confusion. The enemy sometimes attacks me with dreams. The other night I dreamt that the whole movement would become immoral, that people would be found out for their sin. All night long the enemy told me I had nothing to say to people. Then I woke up at 4.30am trying to remember who it was who was immoral. I went for a walk and a jogger came by saying 'I would sure like to hear that story again from last night.' I had to walk and pray and repent. It was with me all day, the feeling of impending disaster. Eventually it wore off. Those are the kinds of battles you will fight.

When I take out teams, I try to get them to experience as much as possible, because God has shown me that we will send out teams all over the world. We have to start here, with our local church teams.

THE PATTERN OF THE CHURCH OF JERUSALEM

The church at Jerusalem functions as a pattern for church planting.

Pastors often pray for a great harvest. But what would you do if you had 3000 converts tomorrow? Who would pastor them? So, you need to have a group of disciples first. The early church had to have a model to follow, just like Jesus was the model to the twelve and the seventy.

1. Jesus saw in the Twelve the beginning of the true Church, the true Israel, his new creation (Galatians 6:15–16).

2. He viewed them as the twelve patriarchs, or the fathers of the Church. They had been trained, prepared, instructed and empowered (Acts 1,2,3 & 8).

3. They were called to lead in the carrying out of the great commission (Matthew 28:18–20).

   They were a well-trained leadership ministry team planted in Jerusalem before the great outpouring. They knew how to cast out demons and pray for the sick. They had a whole set of teaching from Jesus.

   We spent three years building a core. When we started this church we did not tell them what we were doing. We spent a lot of time with people, eating sandwiches with them, taking them with us on trips. We would just meet and worship. How do you make a worshipper? You just bring them into a group of worshippers! How do you teach someone to pray for the sick? You take someone's hands and place it on the sick person and say 'speak to it.' They say, 'how do you do that?' 'Mr. bone ... ?'

When I was doing ministry in Forth Worth there was a young man called David Hall who was hit by the Holy Spirit, overcome for almost two days. When I came back to Forth Worth I watched him and his friends. Those kids were dangerous! The people were Baptists. These five boys would converge on someone, then the person would hit the floor. They put their hands on a blind person. They said, 'In the name of Jesus see.' They were having such fun. They were just boys. Wow, will they have fun when school opens!

I remember Shannon, Bob's daughter. She said, 'I want to receive the Holy Spirit.' She asked big questions. Then, after much discussion, she said, 'I am ready.' Then over a few months all her friends came over. So many were healed, touched, and saved. The kingdom is for everyone.

4. A large base was built up in urban Jerusalem that immediately began meeting in houses, then in the temple, in Solomon's colonnade. They gathered for congregational meetings and celebration meetings (Acts 2:46; 3:11; 4:31; 5:12).

This was incredible church growth. Who would run the nursery? They had 3000, then another 5000, counting men only. They probably went from 120 to about 20,000 in three months. Where are you going to park the camels? Where are we going to meet? There had to be some disciples there first to see to it all. So, we may not have great growth because we do not have enough disciples. I believe that God will double our church next year, here, in this building.

5. The believers met to break bread, share fellowship, pray and receive teaching from the apostles and ministry teams. They must have spent time just swapping Holy Spirit stories. 'Peter did this.' 'John did that!' People would say, 'I would love to do that.' The answer would be, 'You will, just hang around with them.'

6. They delegated administrative responsibilities to others to give themselves time for their own personal ministries.

The way I spend my time now is very different from the way I spent my time at the beginning of this church. Now, I spend time with Vineyard Ministries International and other ministries, but in the beginning all my time was taken up training the core. This growth was predicated on the fact that there were people who were ready for the growth.

As far as I know, there is not a single act of evangelism in the New Testament that is not accompanied by signs and wonders. It was a base for a flow of manpower and ministry development. Barnabas, Stephen and Philip were trained there. Then persecution scatted the disciples throughout the region. They were discipled in teachings and basic practices. These are the building blocks. Whatever you are, they will become. He is our model. Out of him comes a group of people like him. Then we can build a church on that. Often we gather disaffected people out of other churches. They will come and be disgruntled with you. Don't be in a big hurry to gather such people. The key is building disciples from those you have won.

WHO CAN I LEAD?

Who can I make disciples of? Another issue to consider in selecting your target group and area is, who will follow me as their leader? There are five types of people that will respond to you.

Five groups of people

1. People like you! People you can relate to. Would you choose that person as a friend? Do I want to spend time with these people?

2. Good prospects are people that God has prepared to 'do what the Father is doing.' You become a disciple and you will find there are many people waiting for you. When they see someone else doing what they have dreamed about doing, they will just want to jump in. They want to do what you are doing. I am really enjoying what I am doing. I like doing this stuff. It is the most fun I have ever had. I don't have to work hard to get to do it. And I find I don't have to work hard to get other people to do it, if I am doing what I really like to do. Enjoy what you are doing! Ask people, 'Do you

want to do the stuff.' Do what you are and do it with all your heart. Then you will find people who want to do it with you.

3. People who voluntarily follow you. Never recruit. Never try to talk people into it. I try to focus on following Jesus, then when I look back, I notice people who are coming along. Never spend time recruiting people, trying to make them want to do it.
4. People you prove your leadership. You lead by knowing the next step, or even by recognizing who the leader is. You prove leadership by leading. It is not a position.
5. People you have ministered to. (Authority comes through service). If you have really helped people, they will go with you. If you don't really help people, there will not be a crowd following you.

Do what you are!

EQUITY SCALE

An important issue in how fast a church will develop is your existing equity in a community. An equity scale is measured by the percentage of people you have that are:

- Interested in you
- Interested in what you are doing
- Willing to commit to what you are doing.

You can go to some places and they don't know Jesus, or Vineyard, or you, or anything. In other places they may know all of the above. A lot of people will dialogue with you.

One brother in Calvary went to Pittsburgh. He had been raised there, then he went to Vietnam, then he got into drugs, then he got saved. Then God sent him back where he came from. He went back to his Mum. Then he went to visit all his old friends. He went to their parties, his friends and his brother's friends. Then he told them about Jesus. God started meeting people. Soon he had 600 people. The local pastor's association wanted to meet him. They asked, 'Who trained you?' 'Who ordained you?' 'What denomination are you from?' He did not know how to answer them. A whole lot of his kids were with him. Finally, he said to the pastors, 'you don't understand. Have you received the Holy Spirit since you were saved?' Then he called the kids in and asked the Holy Spirit to come on them. They were hit by the power of God. Then he said to the pastors, 'you have the papers, but you don't have the power.'

God is moving today. Kids see it and say, 'hey let's go do that!'

What about those who are only slightly interested? Let them move on. 'Adios. I have not got time to argue you into what I am doing.' I spend none of my time trying to convince people. If people do not respond, I am on my way.

OVERVIEW OF THE BUILDING PROCESS

PHASE I: GATHERING

Personal Evangelism—people meeting exercises

Think about anything that will help you meet people. A young couple was moving from here to plant a church in another city. I told them, 'if all your contacts run dry, do this. Go to your supermarket on Sunday, stand at the baby food counter, and introduce yourself to every young couple that visits the counter.' Young couples with babies have a great need to be in relationships with other young couples with babies. Young couples have interest, energy and time, and a high social focus. Make up something, some reason to meet them. 'Hi, we live in the area, and we are starting a class for young couples from the area. Are you interested?' You will be feeding into a high level of interest. Most people are looking for relationship. Those who are new to the area are the most susceptible. You could think of other counters to stand at.

I have a friend who had a 'grits' method. He started about 10 churches in the Chicago area. He would stand at the grits counter. He said every person who stood at that counter was a Southern Baptist. You have got to meet people! You will not meet them in front of the tube. Our problem is that we work too hard on too few. We gather a few people and we throw everything we have on them. It is premature. Someone was flattering me the other day. I said, 'on an average Sunday we have about 200 first time visitors. Of those, about 100 come back more than once, and about 50 eventually stay. That means 3 out of 4 do not stay. There is something they do not like. This is reality. Of the fifty that stay for a while, half of them do not stay more than a year. Not everybody stays!' However, over a few months I want at least a 1000 of them to stay. I want to get the front door far enough from the back door to have a crowd. Amongst them, there will be a core that are disciples.

OVERVIEW OF THE BUILDING PROCESS

Felt need seminars or groups

A felt need seminar could be potty training classes for young mothers. We build a large church on that ministry in Yorba Linda. Many young families lived out there in a ten-year period. So, I met with young wives and asked them their 10 top needs, and that is how we came on the idea of potty training. We ran them for five years. We had hundreds who came to the class, and many converts.

Or you could offer a course on how to buy a house. Interest rates are high right now. Or you could offer a course on how to budget, or how to handle stress. All you are looking for is a basis for relationship with them.

Building relationships and inviting to groups (i.e. discovery groups)

Advertising

I have seen the use of media that has worked in various parts of the country. Advertise to non-believers through the secular media. Remember they do not watch Christian media.

To reach unchurched believers you can use the Christian media.

Determine your target group

Once you have determined your target group, then you must be continually enlarging your group. Reach out to the many and disciple the few. In the first few years, gather, gather, gather! Young people like cheap fun, beach outings, mountain outings, athletic activities, or church get-togethers to talk. They like anything that does not cost too much, but gives them an opportunity for social exchange, especially if they are new in the neighborhood.

A young girl in our church had this strategy. Whenever new people moved into the area, she would bake fresh bread and give it to them.

Going to the beach or mall is not that effective, because people are still unrelated. But meeting people at work, or across the street is much more personal. The first priority is friends, the next group is near neighbors and work associates. You must be bold enough to talk to people and risk them getting mad at you, or losing your popularity, or even your job.

PHASE II: HOME GROUPS

OVERVIEW OF THE BUILDING PROCESS

Form one or more fellowship groups in your neighborhood

It all depends on the geography. In one church they started one at a college in a girl's dorm, one at work in a big factory, and another one in the neighborhood. The two wives set up a babysitting club and started a group there. This was all in the first three months. None of these groups new each other at first. Then they started them meeting after a few months.

Home groups are where you can build identity

Build identity by sharing your vision. It is impacting if you can tell them how God spoke to you. 'He told me to come and speak to you!' Tell your story over and over again. Why are you here, what are your values? One planter who heard me say this, and then went to plant, came back and said how true it was. He said he had told his story over 2000 times.

Build identity by teaching and modeling your values. Not only tell your story, show your story. Model before them what you want them to be. It is a little like a bus ride. Sometimes a bus driver may change his route. At that point some will get off while others will stay. When some get off, that is fine, let them go. Someone was excited about our kinships. One man asked, 'will there always be kinships here.' I said 'probably not. Some day we may have other kinds of groups.' He said, is that not 'Vineyard.' No, we are about gathering people. It does not matte which vehicle we use for it. Whatever it takes to develop relationship, identity and discipleship; that is all that matters.

Home groups are where you can develop leaders

Begin developing leadership (refer back to the section on discipleship). Discipleship works like this.

- You do it, and they watch you.
- Then they do it and you watch them.
- Then you leave them doing it, etc.

Use this discipleship method in releasing people into leading groups. You will know who they are by looking over your shoulder. Notice the ones that follow you around. They are not always the ones you would pick on your own preference. But pick the ones that always want to be with you in the activity. Then begin to develop relationship with them.

PHASE III: MULTIPLY GROUPS AND A MONTHLY GATHERING OF ALL

Your method should be to,

- Release leaders to lead groups, and
- Create new groups by division, seeding and adoption.

This works in many different ways. Seeding is taking two or three and sending them out to start a new group. Or you take them with you to start a new group. Keep your eyes open and see what God is doing in the community. You can also adopt groups that already exist. Bless them and encourage them.

Develop a sense of mission in your groups. Encourage outreach. You must have some momentum. Anytime the mission and momentum are not congruent, things will not work.

What do you do if you have gone somewhere, worked for ten months and nothing is working? Well, just close it down, move to a new part of town and start again. Just lay it all down and start all over again! That is pragmatism. We can get so lost in the process, or so attached to a small group of people. But the bottom line is, if there isn't a church forming, then back off and start all over again. It is hard, but it can be done. Some of the most powerful churches I know had false starts.

Always provide room for new people to be absorbed. The easiest way is to start new groups. If some groups have become 'primary groups' and do not absorb well, then you have to start new groups. You must constantly have a way in which people can access groups. We have some groups who have decided to not grow. Some of their reasons are OK for a while, but most of the time they justify it with nonsense. Actually, it will go on for a while and then go sour on them. We allow it now and then. But we cannot let that attitude stop the progress of the church. They are good people, but pretty soon the group dies and we have to start those people up in new groups again.

Always be starting new groups. Always be meeting new people. You are in the people processing business! Have you ever seen what they do to carrots, or tomatoes, or potatoes? They come in at one end of our factory and go out at the other end. Our hope is to try and clean them up a little while they move through. We can work with some of them in depth, but most of them not. We are not in the people keeping business. Most pastors think they are. You are always going to have people leaving you, and people joining you. Enjoy the process. The process is of embracing and releasing, again and again. Hopefully you will release better and better quality.

Monthly gatherings of a cluster of home groups will provide enthusiasm. If you have two or three little groups, and you gather them to have picnics and outings and worship, energy will take place. Suddenly we realize we are greater as a whole than as a part of the whole, in our one group. Energy is released. The small group meets one level of needs, for intimacy. The primary need met by the larger group is to build a sense of mission. Next time we gather there are six groups, not four. This gives a sense of mission, or 'otherliness.'

Arrange training events in various ministry areas. Begin the discipleship process. They need to learn to worship, to pray, to study the word, to be married, etc. etc. This covers the basic practices of discipleship you want to train them in. Train leaders without telling them you are doing it. Don't say, 'I will make you an elder.' Never say that. Elders are only elders when they 'eld.' Only God can do that. You can never make one by giving them a label. They spell 'elder' 'b-o-s-s.' We have hundreds of elders with the function, but not the title. It took me twenty years to figure this out. Just quit calling them elders, and they will be elders.

PHASE IV: DEVELOP WEEKLY CELEBRATIONS

Once you have operated on the basis of weekly small group meetings and monthly gatherings of the small groups, the time comes when you must move to weekly meetings where the whole body comes together for worship, teaching and body ministry. The event could be mid-week, or on Sunday nights. Do not, if you can help it, start on Sunday mornings. If you do, you have all the expectations that a mature church can give. They begin to compare you with big churches. If they ask, 'What should we do on Sunday morning?' answer: 'sleep.' If they ask, 'What will I do with my tithe?' answer them: 'Give it to me!' When we meet on Sunday nights, then you can give then.

How do you know when it is time to move to this stage? When you sense the commitment of their time, energy and money. Commitment is spelt 'm-o-n-e-y.' Ask yourself, 'Can we support a facility adequate to the need for a weekly gathering? You can only rent a weekly facility when you have the income to do so. If not, then fall back to a monthly gathering, keep growing small groups, and keep meeting informally until you have enough people and enough income to move to the next stage. But do not succumb to the pressure to have a weekly meeting just to look like a real church. Only do this when you are really ready for it.

Ask, do we have sufficient workers and leaders to run the necessary programs involved in a weekly meeting? (i.e. nursery, children's program, worship leader, etc.). Only start such a program when you have enough, or almost enough personnel. There will come a time when you know it is the next logical step. All churches grow at different rates. Children are like that. Churches are the same. So you have to make qualitative measurements on the level of responsibility your people are giving. Some leaders are too heavy handed in trying to get responsibility out of people. In our church we actually seldom talk about money. Now God has told me 'it is time' to speak about it. We have hundreds of converts who are now ready to hear this.

PHASE V: DEVELOP CONGREGATIONAL UNITS

Here are some possible types:

- Units of home fellowships meeting together (100–300). This fall we will organize our church to have regional congregational meetings. I think it is very advisable to have sub-units in a church.
- Age group fellowships (i.e. twenties), college students, etc.
- Sunday School classes.
- Specialty groups (i.e. singles). Singles groups are functional for education, but be careful about this. Don't put all the singles together. You can have outings for them, or give them special information, but don't have ongoing groups with unmarrieds, to reinforce their loneliness. In a healthy small group it does not matter whether you are married or single.

SUMMARY

If the church planter has the ability to gather many people almost immediately, either due to a high equity in the community or the adoption of an existing group, the process will be altered. If he begins in Phase IV, then he must go back and include the activities of phases 1–III in his infrastructure to create a healthy church.

We are still working on things that I would have liked to have accomplished during the first few years. But for various reasons, one being that we grew fairly rapidly, we did not give them adequate attention. So, if you start a church and it takes off faster than you expect, just go back and work through the stages most other churches work through over a few years.

The following table summarizes the process described above.

Size	Dynamics	Time
0–75	1. Gather to yourself 2. Build identity—define church 3. Need helpers 4. Target limited, i.e. college, career, young marrieds 5. Facility—none	0–6 months
75–150	1. Gather to an identity 2. Leading through workers: recruit, train, deploy, monitor, feed 3. Facility: rent one day per week. Office in home	6 months—1 Year
150–225	1. Gathering 2. Develop leaders—partial transference 3. Target expanding, i.e. College/Career/families/students 4. Continually focus identity 5. Facility: expand adequate to growth	1 year—18 months
225–300	1. Gathering 2. More sophisticated leaders—more training 3. Add workers 4. Facility	18 months—2 years
300–400	1. Continue to gather 2. Define structure of church: family dimension, program definition, i.e. youth groups/Sunday school	3 years
450–600	1. Program definition continues 2. Gather 3. Add leaders and workers 4. Facility	4 years
600–750	1. Fully fledged constituted church	5 years

	2. Target: Cradle to grave	
	3. Gather	
	4. Add leaders and workers	
	5. Facility	

7 Constants:
1. Always looking for God's direction
2. Explain meaning of life—identity
3. Adding to community—gathering
4. Adding workers: recruit, train, deploy, monitor, feed
5. Adding leaders—same process
6. Always increasing workspace
7. Always adding programs to meet felt needs of community

These diagrams reflect about twenty years of experience in working with churches.

The first 150 are gathered to you. In the beginning they gather to you. After that, they make friends with other people. You need to know the sign on the bus, where you are going. You need to know who you are, to build identity, and gather people to yourself.

At this point you just need workers. 'Lets meet at your house.' Your target is limited. Many people try to generalize too much. In the beginning you cannot try to be a supermarket. You need a neighborhood store, or a street sales point with just a few wares.

When we started, we did not need a youth group, because we were a youth group. I was the oldest person. At that time none of the churches were reaching young people. So that was our target. Now it is changing.

These six-month figures are arbitrary. Some churches grow faster, some slower.

75-150

You have established an identity. People say, 'come to our church.' They say 'come with us, we are having fun.'

Now you have to form workers, and work through those workers to groups of people. You are working through other people. You know the people fairly well up to 150 or 175.

You may want to rent a facility once a week. You still work out of your home. Keep the budget really low. Build identity and relationships. Notice that each stage starts with gathering.

OVERVIEW OF THE BUILDING PROCESS

150-225

Add workers and develop your facility. Notice that you do the same thing at each stage, but you modify slightly as you go along.

Your target is expanding now. Instead of just young marrieds, now you have college students as well. Never tire of telling your story. Use it as a preface to preaching. Repeat your values and priorities, then preach.

Remember at 80% of capacity in your venue you are more than full. Keep working with that rule of thumb.

Develop leaders. Some leaders you transfer authority to. Your target develops. Because you now have college and career people, with families, you now need a nursery and a preschool, because your group is more diverse.

Keep emphasizing identity. This is who we are, this is where we are going.

225-300

Now you must lift the level of training. They do not need to know how to recruit, train and deploy when you are doing that. But now that you have 100 or 200 workers you need help to recruit/train/deploy. Later on, you will need to have help in training those who train them.

300-400

Now you need leaders who can train others. Your facility should be full time by then, perhaps a lease.

450-600

At this stage you need more and more program definition. When you have a small village, you don't need a main street. When you get 2000 people you need a stoplight. When you get 20,000 people you need a whole traffic system. Organization is only needed as your organism grows. Some of our hippie converts do not like this stage, because we have to organize better. It feels tight to them. But the church was small when they joined. If we do not organize, they will run over each other the whole time. Those who object to organization and leave will be a blessing to other churches. They have a lot to share. I never feel bad about people leaving.

600-750

Do these basic things, all the time.

SEVEN CONSTANTS

1. *Adding to community—gathering.* We are still adding. How big should this church grow? I really do not care. It is God's church. It is already bigger than I wanted it to be. It has met my needs a while back. But God may want it to be a lot bigger than I want. It is his church, so we just keep going until he shows us differently.
2. *Adding workers*: recruit, train, deploy, monitor, feed. We now have some staff that spend almost all their time in training, in recruit/train/deploy/monitor/feed. That is their full-time job. This is what we discuss in every staff meeting when we gather. We grow the body from the skeleton out. Every bone is the number of workers. The flesh is the people, the crowd.
3. *Always increasing workspace.* We are always adding workers, so we always need more space.
4. *Always adding programs to meet felt needs of community.* The felt needs of the community is determined by the needs of both those outside and those inside our church.

The following diagram helps clarify the way we think about the rate of growth of a given church plant.

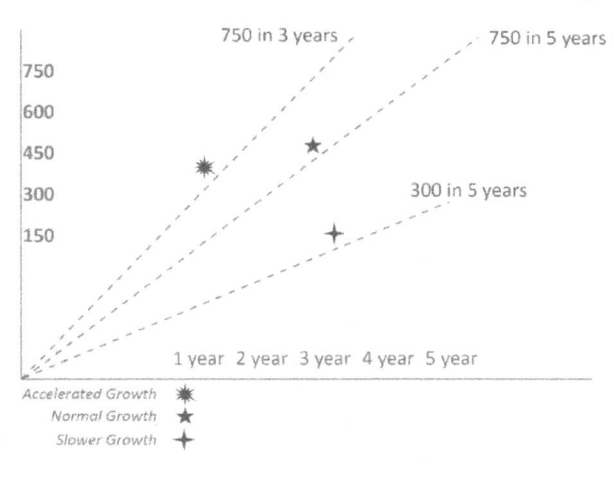

The need for 6 month focuses moves with the growth

Accelerated Growth ✷
Normal Growth ★
Slower Growth ✚

The rate of growth is directly related to population mass, demographics, your skills, and God's blessing. The demographics determine the human material you get, and therefore how fast you can train workers. In some areas the low percentage of 'together' type people will make it difficult to train workers. In other areas where you have healthy families you can develop infrastructure more rapidly. This chart is a rough and crude explanation of the process. In each place the rate will be different.

THE BUILDING PROCESS

The previous section gave an overview of the process. This section will now examine the same process in more detail. The point here is not that you should slavishly follow this procedure. Each church is unique. The idea is to provide you with a conceptual grid through which you can plot and evaluate your progress.

PHASE I: TO ESTABLISH CORE GROUPS

Objectives: To establish an environment in which people can:

1. *Develop personal relationships.* Build significant and meaningful friendship, where people feel it is safe to be real.

2. *Learn to minister to one-another's needs.* This skill will be acquired primarily through modeling. As a demon manifests itself, you show how to do it. At that point those who watch and participate get to do 'demon 101.' As a sickness presents itself, you model on healing. Model as you go. The Holy Spirit will lead the group into the adventure of experiencing God. They will experience things and then get educated. In our society we have reversed that process, and it has not worked that well for us. We should rather adopt the 'show and tell' model. You do the activity, then you explain what you are doing. You do not have to figure out a six-month curriculum. 'First we do the book of Romans—that will take three years.' Some are so onto 'doctrinal soundness,' but what exactly does that mean?

3. *Become intimate with and accountable to each other.* If you have a group with real mutual accountability you are blessed of God. You have, in embryo, the seeds of a whole church. Whatever you plant is what you harvest. If you have a pulpit in a room of six people, or have a whole band for six people, to 'do church' it is crazy. That

is not what you want in small groups. Be a person. Be one of the people in the group. If you really are the leader, it will show. You do not have to have a sign on your chest saying, 'I am the leader.' The leader is shown as needs manifest. The person who knows the next step is the leader.

Process: *These objectives will be accomplished by:*

People-finding experiences

- Making personal contacts in the community.
- Making personal contacts within the Christian community and parachurch organizations.
- Media exposure (concerts, radio, etc.). That is not my personal focus, but it can work. My focus is to develop relationships. That is how we built this church. It is slower. But I had equity in this area. I played at so many gigs. I had music students. I had a recording studio. Probably about 50,000 people knew me by name. I have lived here a long time.

'People-developing' experiences (groups organized)

- Assumptions will be clarified by:
  - *Leadership defining 'who we are.'* Tell your story, again and again.
  - *Participants displaying 'what we want.'* Some like all we do, some only like some things we do, and want to dialogue about what they want in the church. We let them have their preference, but do not let them slow down the progress of the church. Some like gifts, some only some gifts. Do not let debates of such issues side-track your progress.
- Nature of group meetings clarified
  - *Duration/purpose* (how long will we meet? Why will we meet?). If you answer those questions you give people easy access. We will meet at that center for mothers and babies, and it will be for so long, and this is what we will talk about. You always define the duration and process. Start

on time and end on time.
- o *Context/content* (what kind of group will it be? What will we do in the group?). If you are definitive at that point, it will solve lots of problems. Then people can make an easy decision.
- General considerations
  - o Time limits should be clear.
  - o The purpose should be clear.
  - o The leaders should know when they will evaluate.
  - o 'We will give this group six-weeks, then we will evaluate.' You have a different agenda to theirs. If the group is into potty training, your priority is to gather people and disciple them. Their priority is to potty train. If they do not like the Jesus thing, then say to someone, 'from this point on, you are Mrs. Potty training. I am going to move on.'

People-relating experiences

- Provide a climate where relationship building occurs.
- Provide a climate where vision options can be explored.

Evaluation in progress

We know we are ready to move to Phase II when we observe that:

- Intimacy has increased and is being verbalized and demonstrated by the group. 'This is a wonderful group, I am finding my best friends here.'
- Voluntary interaction is occurring apart from organized meetings. They are becoming friends, meeting for coffee, inviting one another to their homes.
- Level of sharing moves from being physical/circumstantial to being spiritual/emotional/interpersonal.

What does the New Testament say about the Phase I objectives and process?

I encouraged you to do the following simple bible study. You can use this study for yourself, or use it in training others. The main thing is that it gives you a key to evaluate.

Reference Summary	Application: What behavior/activity would implement and apply this?
Acts 2:42	
Acts 4:32	
Acts 4:33-34	
Gal.5:13	
Gal.6:2	
Rom.15:1-2	

Plan of action phase 1

Who?	What?	When?	Where?

PHASE II: ESTABLISH A 'CARING COMMUNITY'

Objectives: To provide an environment where participants can

- *Receive and grow in the use of spiritual gifts.* Even in churches that teach about gifts, most people do not actually get to practice. Once again, the thing is modeling, not just teaching. I do not teach about it formally, I just do it to them. I talked to a seminary Professor the other day who was a cessationist. He began to discuss his theological issues with me. As we talked, I started having words of knowledge about his secret sins and issues. It did not take long to convince him that gifts are for today. So, we are not into opinions, or debates. I do not spend time trying to convince people, I just do it to them. I decided to just believe it and obey it. When people come and say 'I want to dialogue about something' I immediately start praying and asking God about them. We are into kingdom business. That cessationists actually need is to be delivered from the bondage of continual assessment, this great preponderance of thought. 'Lets think about this some more,' while people are going to hell all around them. There is no time for dialogue. Let's just do it!

- *Modeling.* Do it, release people to do it themselves, and then give people permission to fail. Someone may think they have a prophecy. Tell them, 'just say it.' 'What if I will be wrong?' 'So what, we can only tell if you just give it, and if it is wrong, no one will die.'

- *The people have their spiritual, emotional and social needs met.* You will never meet all their needs. Having some of them met will keep them coming.

- *Develop an increasing willingness to make friends.* There is a correspondence about feeling good about yourself and their openness to meet other people.

- *Develop an increasing level of intimacy.* This is done through self-disclosure. A lot of pastors put on this aura of professionalism, while they are actually in a mess. To do this is to be a hypocrite. You are not the 'answer man.' You are not 'God's man for the hour.' Someone said on TV, 'John Wimber is the most anointed man in the world today'. I almost vomited. I am just a fat man trying to get to heaven. That's what I am. Someone grappling with the word of God, trying to treat his wife nice, get to know his grandchild, and keep his car going. But I am also in touch with the kingdom of God. There is only one hero here, Jesus Christ! Let's quit lifting up men. Ask their wives, who have to wash their underwear.

You develop intimacy by self-disclosing. I cannot live with the religiosity that is among us. I hate religion. I hate it passionately. All of us are tainted with it. We need to root it out. It is manifest when we try to be, or appear to be, something that we are not.

Process: These objectives will be accomplished by

- *Providing an opportunity for gifts of the Spirit to be modeled, released and practiced.* When I wrote this ten years ago, it was for a group that planted 50 churches using this model. They used mostly young couples. My theology about gifts is that Christians have them in them, but we just need to release them.

- *Providing times for learning to live together* (retreats, campouts, etc.). Don't forget to have fun! It is very helpful to go away for weekends from time to time. It builds intimacy. Don't build an atmosphere in the church that we are all under a 'great burden of God' or the idea that works of the Spirit only occur 'at the altar.' God words at camps and in homes and in public places, just as much, or perhaps more, than he does in formal gatherings. One of our members walked into a restaurant where a man had palsy and was struggling to eat his breakfast. This guy never went to church before he came to us, so he thinks everything I say is the truth—poor man. So, he just walked up to the palsied man and said, 'you don't have to shake like that. In the name of Jesus be healed.' The man instantly stopped shaking. Then he started talking to him. 'Let me tell you about who healed you.' We don't know what we have got here. It is fun stuff!

- *Providing socially non-threatening and informal times to establish new relationships.* We must create an environment where new people do not feel threatened. We should be continually inviting new people in and be secure enough in what God is doing to welcome whoever may come. Some guy down the street is a pastor and wants to come to your group. Maybe he will steal your people? Let him come. One man in our group, who was a Lutheran pastor, asked to teach on infant baptism. I said sure. He asked, 'is it what you believe.' I said no, just tell the people that John has a different view before you start. Don't be threatened. If everyone left here and went over there, what would I do? I would go there myself. I want to be where God is working. This is not my church.

- *Providing opportunities to deepen the level of intimacy.* One of the ways to do this is to help people through a crisis. As soon as a group has walked through a crisis with someone, they will be bonded together.

- *Providing opportunities to talk about the next phase.* From time to time, you say, 'here is where I think we will go next. I read a book, and I think this is where we are going.' You don't have to pretend to be more mystical than reality.

THE BUILDING PROCESS

Evaluation of progress

We know that we are ready to move to Phase III when we observe that:

- Members are receiving, expressing satisfaction with, and growing in the use of spiritual gifts.
- Members are expressing freely that their needs are being met by the group at all levels (spiritual, emotional, persona, social).
- New members are being exposed to and readily absorbed into the group.
- Members continue to freely express intimacy in areas of spiritual need. If you see that happening, then you have a good indicator.

What does the New Testament say about the Phase II objectives and process?

Reference Summary	Application: What behavior/activity would implement and apply this?
Rom.1:11–12	
Rom.12:6	
Rom.15:7	
1 Pet. 4:9–10	
Heb.13:16	
James 5:16	
1 John 1:7	

Plan of Action: Phase II

Who?	What?	When?	Where?

The 'who' may be certain group leaders that you will train for the next phase. 'What' is the training you will do. 'When,' is what dates have you set? 'Where' is the venue.

PHASE III: ESTABLISH GROUP MULTIPLICATION

Objectives: To establish an environment where people can

- Develop a sense of mission, which will result in a desire to reach out to others. It comes as a by-product of feeling better about themselves and feeling intimate. Our culture is very generous. People want to give things away. Set goals for quality, and it will produce quantity.
- Create new groups through divisions, seeding and adoption.
- Discover who is especially skilled at receiving new people.
- Put individuals who have natural ability in evangelism, or a special ministry ability, in touch with others who need it (evangelism/intimacy).

Process: These objectives will be accomplished by

- *Keeping effective models visible* (Telling stories of past victories). I tell stories all the time of people who are succeeding. They are very motivating. Tell stories of the things that are working, or not working.
- *Through division, seeding, and adoption, provide room for new people to be absorbed.* You are always meeting new people and always starting new groups. Some have said things like this to me. 'I have been here for eight months, I have fifty people and they are not that keen to grow.' My advice is, 'then hand them over to someone you have trained and go build another group of fifty.' The one thing we must do is build a church. You also need to be able to survive. I have got to sustain. So, you must know how to set boundaries. Get your rest, have time with your families. You must be here next week. There will always be people who have more needs than you can meet. So, you must know how to sustain. Nothing they put on you can afford to stop you. This one thing we must do, is build the church! As we build the community, eventually it can do far more than I could ever do on my own. Our priority is to meet needs, but the higher priority is to build a church, so that it can meet peoples' needs.
- *Providing modeling and training on 'how to be friends' to help with*

the absorption of new members. As your church grows you will find an inevitable tension will begin to emerge. These will require you to change your role. You cannot keep the level of intimacy you had with people in the beginning. It is difficult on you and on them. In the recent past I have not spent much time with some of the original people who started this church with me, who are my close friends. In the last year I think I have gone out to dinner once with friends like that. I have attended far more events with pastors and leaders. I do not like that, neither do they. Some could not go through that transition, so they left. But I must build the church.

- *Encouraging group members to reach out to their families and others in their sphere of influence.* When people are bringing their neighbors and friends, then you have something.

Evaluation of progress

We know we are ready to move to Phase IV when we observe that:

- New members are being added regularly to groups.
- The number of groups is increasing.
- Group members are expanding their outreach into their individual spheres of influence. When you see someone bringing people from work, or their neighbors, then you are into 'pay dirt.' You have a disciple. They are ready to risk in relationships. Then you know you have something. You do not have much until you get to that place.
- Relational skills are being refined. They are becoming more and more able to love people.

What does the New Testament say about the Phase III objectives and process?

Reference Summary	Application: What behavior/activity would implement and apply this?
John 4:35	
1 Thess.1:8	
2 Tim.2:2	
James 2:1	
Mt.5:16	
1 Pet.2:9	

Plan of Action: Phase III

Who?	What?	When?	Where?

PHASE IV: ESTABLISHING CONGREGATIONS

Objectives: To establish an environment in which

- The multiplied groups come together for fellowship on a congregational level.

- Ministries can be developed that meet the felt needs of the community. Now you are becoming 'otherly.' Up to this point the church was inward looking. Now they have relationship and identity, and an understanding of basic skills. Now they are ready to help others. They can clean up somebody's house, or help indigent people, or pick up people and bring them to church.

- There is on-going penetration of the unchurched community. Witnessing is ongoing, not necessarily by handing out tracks, but by people telling their friends, 'I am having a great time.' They say, 'what are you sniffing or drinking.' You say, 'we have this group where we share and we pray.' 'You pray?' 'Yes.' This is when you are naturally confident to talk about your faith.

Groups receive those reached through mass penetration.

Process: These objectives will be accomplished by

- Assessing the multiplied groups (congregations) needs for fellowship, worship, teaching and facilities. How many groups do we have? Are the facilities necessary? Most of our people have two events a week, on Sunday and one mid-week event. We do not have all sorts of committees like many churches. So they have time.

- Developing appropriate solutions for meeting congregation's needs.

- Recognizing congregational leaders. By that I do not mean naming them and giving them a title. You just get alongside them and ask them to help in something. Don't put official titles and structures on people. It kills people. Don't do that. Just ease into things.
- Surveying the community to identify felt needs which the congregation might minister to. A couple of years ago we refurnished about a hundred homes in Orange Country, for indigent people. The purpose of the exercise was to make our congregation 'otherly.' That is the Christian life.
- Providing training in various types of ministry.
- Experimenting with programs designed to penetrate a specific group in the community.
- Providing encouragement and training for group members to enable them to absorb those reached through community outreach programs.

All these are just ideas. You do not have to have them all.

Evaluation of progress

We know that we are ready to move to Phase V when:

- The process outlined above is operating to the satisfaction of the congregation. Their satisfaction will be evidenced by:
  - The commitment of their time,
  - The commitment of their energy,
  - The commitment of their money.

  This is how you know they like it. There is always a ratio between workers and people attending. For every worker there are about four people attending. We have about 5,000 attend every Sunday. We have about 1,000 workers. I have noticed the same ratio everywhere I have been. So, if we want to double our members, we need 2,000 workers.

- There is a sense that the congregation is being pulled ahead by the activities rather than a sense that they are pushing the activities along (Freight train versus snowplow). There is that feeling of being drawn, rather than working hard. God is working with us, speaking to us. Everything is greased, it is easy!

THE BUILDING PROCESS

What does the New Testament say about the Phase IV objectives and process?

Reference Summary	Application: What behavior/activity would implement and apply this?
Acts 2:41–42	
Acts 2:46	
Acts 2:47	
Gal.6:10	
Mark 16:15,20	
Mt.18:19–20	
Acts 20:20	

Plan of Action: Phase IV

Who?	What?	When?	Where?

PHASE V: ESTABLISHING CELEBRATION

Objectives: To provide a way to

- Discover and develop an appropriate style of celebration. What is appropriate for you? Some like a rock band. Some say, 'it would not be a Vineyard if it had an organ.' Yes it would. Do what works for you. If you want 43 mandolins, then do it. Don't tie yourself into our programs. Tie yourself into the philosophy.
- Recognize and/or affirm pastoral leadership.
- Assess facility needs (lighting, heat and air, nursery, parking, location, times).
- Obtain necessary recognition and tax-exempt status. I do not live easily with this, because I want freedom from the government, but I am still thinking about it.

Process: These objectives will be accomplished by

- Exploring, experimenting and evaluating format options for specific celebration needs. We have a laid-back style, which is appropriate to our needs. If you are reaching the baby boom generation then take a careful look at what you do. But if you are not, then it may not fit. Things are also different in different regions.
- Clarifying everyone's responsibilities, authority, and relationships.
- Following a planning process, which includes exploring and choosing facilities.
- If necessary, remain alert to the need to acquire land and/or permanent facilities. Our encouragement is to avoid getting tied up with building projects. Our world is full of monuments. They tend to become the highest priority, higher than the priority of the expansion of the church. Buildings also make you inflexible. Banks move with the people flow, so they keep moving. Gandhi said, 'there go my people, I must catch up with them, for I am their leader.'

Evaluation of progress

We know we have completed this phase when:

- The process outlined above is operating to the satisfaction of the congregation.
- Their satisfaction will be evidenced by:
    - The commitment of their time,
    - The commitment of their energy,
    - The commitment of their money.
- There is a sense that the congregation is being pulled ahead by their celebration activities.

What does the New Testament say about the Phase V objectives and process?

Reference Summary	Application: What behavior/activity would implement and apply this?
1 Cor.14:23,26	

THE BUILDING PROCESS

Rom.15:6	
1 Tim.5:22	
1 Tim.3:10	
Mt.6:33	

Plan of Action: Phase V

Who?	What?	When?	Where?

PASTORING A GROWING CHURCH

One of the major problems a pastor in a growing church faces is the issue of role change as the church grows. Firstly, the average pastor has no idea that this needs to happen. What is more, his people will have tension with change because they will interpret it as abandoning their primary relationship. A good illustration of this is when a pastor who, when the church was small, had an 'open study' policy in which people were encouraged to 'drop in' on him, now has to go to an 'appointment only' policy because of the demands on his time. People who have always been able to 'get in' now can't and are often angered by it.

The problem is two-fold.

1. The pastor has had to prioritize the use of his time. A good illustration of this is Moses in the wilderness (Exodus 18:13–27; Deuteronomy 1:9–18). The solution is that he will have to replace himself as Moses did, appointing leadership the people 'can see.' This is often overlooked with a pastor in a growing church.

2. There is the matter of educating the church to this priority so that they will not be frustrated in their desire to get a meaningful audience from someone in authority. A good illustration of this problem is in Acts 6:1–7. The key here is finding qualified manpower that the pastor may transfer to.

You will have noticed in the Acts 6:1–7 text that the apostles committed themselves to the priority of the Word and prayer, and asked the people to find qualified manpower to minister in the area of taking care of the widows' needs. It is important to recognize that this was a delegated responsibility or authority given to the people by the apostles, and not one the people had by rights.

It is also essential to recognize that the people selected highly qualified leadership who, as in the case of Stephen and Philip, distinguished themselves in the ministry.

All of the above may be illustrated graphically in the following way.

Changes in the Pastoral Role

	Stage 1	Stage 2	Stage 3	Stage 4
1000	Shepherd to all	Shepherd to all	Shepherd to all	Shepherd to all
(200)	Personal	Through workers	Through leaders	Through professionals, lay leaders and workers
Leadership Skills	Model	Delegate it	Transfer it (partial)	Transfer it (total)
Comparative Models	Cowhand, Herdsman	Top hand, driver	Cattle foreman, sheep foreman	Cattle rancher, sheep rancher
	Ball-player	Team captain	Coach	General manager

THE STAGES OF DISCIPLESHIP

Your role must be negotiated again and again, as you develop. The graph shows correlations of relationships. There are a lot of problems in most churches in the process of building the staff. In most churches it is near death to be the first associate. Most pastors do not know how to work with another person. There is a great mortality rate with associates. We have yet to develop the training material for associates, and how to build a staff. We have had those who have left here as well.

But this is more about what happens to the senior pastor. He learns to delegate, then to transfer in part, then to do a total transfer. At this stage Sam Thompson is the executive pastor. I no longer marry people or have a lot of contact with the church. Sam really runs the church. Blaine Cook runs VMI. Bob Fulton runs the church planting ministry. So, we have VCF Anaheim, VMI and [what will become AVC]. The purpose in sharing this is to say that I can run quite a few organizations if I don't have to actually run them.

The rancher will not be the person to mend a fence. If it is a major job he will delegate some top hands to delegate to the cowhands. There are those who delegate over those who delegate. The foreman will delegate the top hands, who will then define the work. The top hands job is to run workers. Jobs alter as you go along.

As a pastor in a new church my job was to do everything. Preach, cast out demons, heal the sick, counsel people, bring the food, and organize events. Then you start to delegate. You start to ask people, 'will you bring the sandwiches.' Then I release people who release people.

I have used the following stages as a helpful way to understand the process.

Stage I: Cowhand—Ballplayer—Herdsman

- The pastor models the ministry to wants to multiply (i.e. evangelistic bible studies). He goes to the marketplace, meets people, invites them in, and he teaches the study. Maybe at his house.

- The pastor finds someone who wants to do what he is doing (usually someone he has ministered to in the study). The kind of person who comes early, stays late, asks about commentaries. You can tell by their level of interest.

- The pastor gets the recruit to do it and observes his performance (usually by asking the recruit to 'stand in' for him). If he did it while you were on vacation, you can ask the people, 'how did he do.'

- The pastor trains the recruit on an ongoing 'as needed' basis, leaving the recruit to do the work. This is usually done by the pastor starting a new group or starting a new ministry and leaving the recruit with the old one. Sometimes groups cannot handle that. Sometimes you need to divide it. It all depends on the dynamics of the group.

- The pastor returns periodically to encourage and retrain the recruit and to do more recruiting through him. The recruit will do it 'his' way eventually, but in the process may leave out important things that keep the ministry going. Therefore, it is essential to go back from time to time and retrain the people that you have trained. As they are ministering, they will develop the relationships that make a good recruiting climate, so you must go back and recruit through them, so that you can have access to the people they are ministering to. Some, who were not ready earlier, are now ready.

- The pastor gets a second recruit to minister and observes his performance. The pastor may ask the new recruit to stand in for the seasoned recruit. Then, as above, the new recruit gradually takes on the work, and the seasoned recruit goes on to take over a group from the pastor or starts a new group. You start with one, then two, then three, then one dies, then you add a new one, and on it goes.

- The first-generation members of a group are the hardest to get. It took us nearly a year to get the first seven kinship groups, and three died out of the first seven. Then we called them all back together and had another training event. Then we started another six. So, we went from seven to four to ten. By the third generation it was relatively easy to start groups. Now we had a whole lot of people who knew how kinships worked. By the fourth generation we were starting, in one week, what it took us one year to establish earlier on. Now you have so many people who have been in the process so long.

- The pastor does all the above steps until he has a maximum of twelve functional recruits. If you have twelve groups in your church, averaging between 16–22, you have a functional church, about 220 adults. Add the children and you have 350. Then you are in the upper 5% of churches in the USA. We have about 80 kinships now, plus a few other groups. I know this fall we need about 150. That is not unrealistic.

When we first started healing, I taught on healing every week for months. Now I hardly teach on it, because it is established in the church. It is normative. It has been birthed. The same applies to small groups. They are part of us. Now only the new people need to be exposed to the information, but I do not need to preach about it. I preached on the kingdom every Sunday for a whole year. Now it is birthed amongst us. You do a lot of teaching and work at the start up, then you can just finesse it later on.

Stage 2: Top hand—team captain—driver
- The pastor only models ministry on an 'as needed' basis. He spends most of his time doing the last three steps above.
- The pastor looks for a recruit that can handle an assistant position to him.
- The pastor repeats the first four steps above on the new level for the recruit so that he can learn to do what the pastor has done in terms of recruiting and training workers. Now when you have four or five of those guys, you really have something: people who can produce people who can lead people.

Stage 3: Cattle foreman—coach—sheep foreman
- The pastor now manages the entire system by functioning as a foreman and/or at a coach level. Then, he begins the process of looking for an assistant foreman that could take his place, repeating the training process by clarifying what it is he is doing at that level and then leaving them working the entire system—stages 1 through three.

Stage 4: Cattle rancher—general manager—sheep rancher
- The pastor is now ready to move to another area of ministry in the church by beginning to repeat the entire process. While he is doing so, he must keep in mind that anything that has been started must continue to be managed and therefore, he must come back from time to time and retrain and encourage everything from the worker level, which would be the model cowhand, ballplayer or herdsman on up, so that he can maintain quality as well as quantity in the entire ministry.
- By this stage you may define roles in terms of ministry types, say children's workers, or youth workers, or pastoral workers. At this point in the church we must reorganize the church according to

the workers we have. Let's say you have a Sunday school superintendent who has worked for twenty years. Rather than try to replace that one with one, replace the person with three, none of whom are at the same level of responsibility. You scale down the job into its parts and put people in at various levels.

EFFECTIVE EVANGELISM TODAY

There is voluminous material written on the area of evangelism today. My hope here is to simply give you a practical perspective from my own experience.

There are many ways to do evangelism. Some are very productive and some produce little if any fruit. Let's start by examining some ineffective ways to evangelize in our culture.

INEFFECTIVE METHODS

1. *Street witnessing*—It can sometimes lead to converts, but it very seldom leads to active disciples participating in a local church.
2. *Local newspaper adds*—Take out an ad in the local paper and hang your shingle. A typical approach to evangelism is to rent a facility, advertise, and start weekly meetings. Although this may attract some people, it is by and large ineffective.
3. *Door to door evangelism*—This approach can produce fruit, but there are better ways to use your evangelistic time and energy. First, you are competing with many other messengers using the same method (i.e. the cults). Second, many people resent the intrusion on their privacy and the hard sell approach.

EFFECTIVE METHODS

Relational evangelism

In our culture the message must be packaged in love and friendship. People must know they are cared for before they are ready to accept your message. So, the key to spreading the gospel is building relationships.

- *Bridges*—these are common interests (such as sports, hobbies,

- *Mining the vein*—When a gold miner strikes gold, he will mine the vein until it runs dry. Evangelism can be a similar process. When we lead one person to Christ, we have found a vein to work. Each person we lead to Christ has a network of friends and family that he can lead us into relationship with. A simple way to discover the network is to ask a new believer: 'Who will you share what has happened to you with first?' He will instinctively know who of his friends will be open to the gospel. Then you can offer to go with him to help him share with his friend. This process can lead you to many people.

Power evangelism

A second emerging effective means of evangelism is a visible demonstration of the power of God. In the Acts of the Apostles, one healing led to 3,000 conversions in one instance and 5,000 in another. In the same way we are seeing healings opening the door to evangelism. If a person is touched by the power of God and healed, he will later become a Christian. He has seen the reality of God's love and nearness and naturally responds to the gospel. Also, a healing is a powerful witness to family and friends that will open them to the gospel message.

Felt need evangelism

A third effective means of evangelism has been popularized in Robert Schuler's saying, 'Find a need and fill it.' Anything that meets the felt needs of a community can act as a bridge to sharing Jesus. When people see that the gospel is relevant to their everyday lives and needs, they will be much more responsive. Seminars offered to the community on marriage, personal growth, or parenting, are examples of this method. They bring you into contact with people and build bridges.

CPSIA information can be obtained
at www.ICGtesting.com
Printed in the USA
LVHW041723170322
713616LV00013B/1625